# SHADOW WORK *for* CORE WOUNDS

## Move Beyond Toxic Positivity to Heal Emotional Trauma & Find True Belonging

*Ora North*

REVEAL PRESS

AN IMPRINT OF NEW HARBINGER PUBLICATIONS

## Publisher's Note

Distributed in Canada by Raincoast Books

NEW HARBINGER PUBLICATIONS is a registered trademark of New Harbinger Publications, Inc.

Copyright © 2026 by Ora North
             Reveal Press
             An imprint of New Harbinger Publications, Inc.
             5674 Shattuck Avenue
             Oakland, CA 94609
             www.newharbinger.com

Cover design by Sara Christian
Interior design by Tom Comitta
Acquired by Jennye Garibaldi and Elizabeth Hollis Hansen
Edited by Madeline Greenhalgh
All Rights Reserved

Library of Congress Cataloging-in-Publication Data on file

MIX
Paper | Supporting responsible forestry
FSC
www.fsc.org
FSC® C008955

Printed in the United States of America

28    27    26

10   9   8   7   6   5   4   3   2   1   First Printing

"Truly healing our wounds means inviting all our foul-mouthed monsters to come sit with us; to share their bitter wisdom, no matter how wicked that wisdom may be. Shadow work is gnarly, wild work. It is the work of secrets, the most important work we will ever do. In this book, Ora North expertly maps a journey of integration, a wilderness guide for those seeking a genuine encounter with both the wound and the gift, the fertile dark and the hallowed light that make for a life well-lived."

—**Danielle Dulsky**, author of *The Night House*, *The Holy Wild*, and *Bones & Honey*

"'Shadow work' is a buzz term and seems to be all the rage. The key to shadow work is that it requires just that: work. Folks don't want to do the work. They bypass. Throw love and light at the wound and call themselves healed. Ora has a voice that roars. Shadow Work for Core Wounds does not allow you to bypass your wounds, your shadow, or yourself. Ora breaks down integration and emotional alchemy in a way that is palpable, palatable, and most importantly, practical. You'll be given the tools to face your deepest shadows."

—**Jaclyn Cherie**, creator of Algorithm Magick, folk herbalist, magickal consultant, ordained minister, word alchemist, Usui reiki master, author, and editor at Girl God Books

"Ora, in her signature, magical way, has yet again opened the portal to individual and collective healing. In *Shadow Work for Core Wounds*, she invites us into wholeness by working with the power of archetypes, uprooting our shadow parts, and 'tending to the soil of our souls.' I highly recommend this book for all who are committed to doing their inner work as part of the collective healing needed in these times."

—**Pamela Kowal, MS, LMFT Emeritus**, therapeutic coach, reiki and energy practitioner, and Tarot consultant

"If you need help breaking tenacious, destructive patterns, *Shadow Work for Core Wounds* is the book for you! Ora North offers a grounded, spiritual approach to healing core wounds, while avoiding the toxic positivity that is so rampant in our world. This guided, archetypal journey uncovers common blueprints of human suffering with grace and clarity. Grab your journal and reconnect with your inherent wholeness through this powerful book."

—Trista Hendren, founder of Girl God Books

"Ora North helps us to cut through the carapace of everyday agendas and cut down the sugar of feel-good approaches to self-cultivation to recognize that our deepest soul yearning is for our return from exile and to our soul family and our true place of belonging. She helps us to revisit and understand our wounds as seeds that are planted in the fertile dark, and that, with careful tending, can rise from the mud like the lotus."

—Robert Moss, author of *Conscious Dreaming* and *Dreaming the Soul Back Home*

"Ora North offers a brilliant evolution of shadow work, moving beyond toxic positivity into a deeper cycle of healing. The archetypes of the Self—higher, wounded, compassionate, powerful, primal, creative, and healed—provide an accessible template towards true integration. With various suggestions such as journal reflections, synchronicity, dreamwork, boundaries, and more, this accessible manual becomes a guide to reclaim soul fragments and create a true home within ourselves."

—Nancy Antenucci, speaker, ritualist, lifelong Tarot practitioner, and author of *Psychic Tarot* and *Tarot Rituals*

To every tiny spark of hope within that
almost died, but instead persisted.

# Contents

# *Introduction*

The yearning to belong and feel at home.

This is the most powerful driving force we have. It is also the purest because it reaches into the very core of every human being, into our suffering and our joy. Every healing action, as well as every damaging action, can all be traced back to this yearning. The human spirit is so determined to feel safe, to feel like it belongs, that it can commit great acts of kindness or great acts of atrocities in the name of seeking to feel how it wants to feel.

What is the key difference in whether we create kindness or atrocity? Our relationship to our past wounding and our darker selves. The ways we recognize and acknowledge our yearning, and how we choose to respond to it. That process of acknowledging and working with our wounding and darker selves is what shadow work is, and it's what is necessary to quench our yearning and find our way back home.

I know you're not brand new to personal growth and healing. If you've been drawn to shadow work, I know you've already done a lot of the work. You wouldn't have picked this up if you hadn't. No one comes to shadow work without first being unfulfilled or hurt by the light. The yearning to belong is what first drives seekers to the world of spirituality, after all.

# Unfulfilled Promises

The world of healing and spirituality offers glittering hope, bright balls of white light, and dulcet-toned promises of relief from your suffering. As soon as you enter this world, you are bombarded with affirmations and meditations urging you to think positively in order to overcome any obstacles in your way. We all experience a honeymoon phase with this world. Its optics and its tantalizing rewards easily draw us in, almost as if those promises are enough to soothe our very souls without even working toward fulfilling them yet. Even being in the presence of such hope, such peace and gratitude, has a calming, almost anesthetic effect.

Maybe when you joined your first spiritual community you felt as though you stumbled into the best kept secret in the world, a place where you were a special key to the betterment of humanity, a place where you finally belonged. Maybe you experienced a spiritual awakening of sorts there and have been learning ever since. Maybe you took your first classes on chakras or divination and became enamored with your intuitive abilities and divine mission. Maybe you read a few incredible books on manifestation and healing and instantly felt the foundation of your life shift. You were encouraged to let go, and you did. At least, you let go to the best of your ability. You were instructed to release your negativity and embrace only the positive, and you did, because only embracing the positive felt so much better than continually dealing with those darker parts of you.

Those things improved your life, just as they were designed to do. You probably felt more connected to your soul, and to God or the Universe or however you like to view and name what is sacred to you. You probably noticed that you stood stronger in your truth. Maybe your relationships improved because you understood how to live differently, and you built new friendships with people who were experiencing this as well, which only amplified that sense of belonging.

Perhaps everything in your life improved because of glittering hope and the lovely energies coursing through your body.

But here's the thing about honeymoon phases. They cannot last.

It's not that you didn't put the work in to make it last. You did your vision boards and you recited your positive affirmations and you rejected bad vibes in order to put your energy into more positive things. All those things are beautiful tools, don't get me wrong. But they are gateway tools and maintenance tools, never meant to be the end-all and be-all of true healing and change.

Honeymoon phases in relationships feel as good as they do because we are chemically designed to respond to endorphins and the shiny newness and excitement of it all. It is the same way with any new, beautiful thing, spirituality and healing included. But those chemicals wear off. In our relationships, we are left to see the complicated nest of history and patterns that challenge our compatibility with one another. In spirituality, we are left with the complicated histories and patterns of ourselves, which equally challenge our compatibility with our very existence. When that happens, the feel-good chemicals can no longer cover up or soothe that deep yearning for belonging and home that got you started on your search.

Maybe you eventually noticed that your partnership was getting more and more difficult to maintain, despite the beautiful journey you were on. You and your partner were no longer on the same path, despite your efforts to structure your communication differently, and the contrast of it began to clash again and again. The triggers that once arose on occasion became a frequent occurrence, and what started as an idea for a fresh start in shared healing became an exercise in walking on eggshells.

Focusing on the positive created a beautiful bubble for you, for a time. But the reality of the world and what was happening within it constantly pushed against your bubble, threatening to pop it with each new current event. Perhaps your answer was to fortify your bubble even more, desperately attempting to keep the outside *outside*. I'm not going to lie to you—the bubble feels better than reality. Of course it does. But eventually you realized the boundaries you created were a stone wall that kept you entirely disconnected from the world outside. Did your friends and family slip away somehow? Did your compassion for suffering and your ability to see it get pushed away among whispers to create your own reality? Did your ability to help others suddenly become narrow and isolated, as if you could only help people who were also in that bubble with you? You knew something was off.

You noticed that the more you worked on your meditations, the more you heard a tiny voice crying out inside your head. A voice that was suffering, a voice that held every pain and trauma you'd ever experienced. This was a voice that your spiritual communities and your books perhaps told you to ignore. "Don't give your attention and energy to it," they may have said. "Doing so will only embolden it." So you did what they said, but the more you ignored the voice, the more it ate away at you from the inside. It ate away at your sense of peace and the almost-numbing joy of spirituality you once experienced. Maybe it even started causing bad things to happen in your life, things involving patterns that you thought you had let go of forever. *I thought I was done with this*, you may have observed when a pattern came up time and time again.

While positivity initially empowered you to recognize the control you had over your life, a shadow side to that idea of complete control emerged. It forced you to be responsible for every negative feeling and experience you've had, pushing the ideology into victim blaming and bypassing your pain. Not only did you not receive the world of peace and freedom that you were promised, but it was also *your fault* that you didn't.

Perhaps you were open about your struggles and concerns, but your questions were met with rejections like these: "You're just not manifesting properly." "You're choosing low vibrations." "You are trapped in your

victimhood and haven't evolved enough yet." "You aren't letting it go."
"You are letting your suffering control you." Perhaps you even believed
those things, since they seemed to match the ideals you first fell in love
with when you entered the spiritual world. As a result, you found yourself
in a state of unbelonging. Something was wrong with *you*, not them. *You*
were the weak link in the chain. Unfortunately, if you reached this point
in the journey, you may have been abandoned by the same people who
promised you belonging in the beginning. Not only did this create intense
whiplash from the highs of positivity you were once riding, but it also
stirred up feelings of shame and guilt. The ordeal took away the feeling of
home you were just starting to experience again and contributed to an
eerie underlying thought: *Maybe I just don't belong anywhere.* If this
describes your experience, there is absolutely nothing wrong with you. In
fact, something is very *right* with you, as you're already tuned into the
deeper parts of yourself that yearn to be witnessed and validated, that
yearn to belong and be at home. That yearning for belonging and home
is connected to your core wounds, which are the most important wounds
to examine and work on if you want to heal.

## What Are Core Wounds?

Core wounds are the original pain points of your life. They are the
first seeds of doubt that were planted in the soil of your existence.
They are the blueprints of your emotional suffering. Some people can
pinpoint a singular event in their childhood as a core wound, but we
all have a collection of them. Core wounds were created when you
were rejected or abused or betrayed or were made to feel small for the
first time. Oftentimes, many core wounds will follow the first one in
a similar pattern. For example, if the first core wound you can remember was being abandoned by a loved one, you likely have experienced
a pattern of being abandoned multiple times throughout your life.

That initial core wound sets the tone and creates the blueprints, and every experience you have after that will either affirm or deny that wound. This is why the environment you grew up in has a massive impact on whether the initial wound becomes better or worse as your life continues.

We will explore many different versions and manifestations of your core wounds. But all core wounds, including betrayal and rejection and abandonment, trace back to one wound: the wound of exile. Exile is the forceful separation of a person from their home. When used in an emotional and spiritual way, exile can take many forms. Think of it like this: When your soul is whole, connected to whatever greater force creates meaning and peace, it is at home. That is your soul's natural state and where it belongs. But the human experience is filled with brokenness and misunderstanding. Early on in life, that connection you naturally have to wholeness, to home, is severed. Whatever circumstance first severed your connection to home will always be a painful theme for you to work on throughout your life.

Even beyond this original exile from the wholeness of your soul, exile reappears in many other forms as well that build upon your wounding. Experiencing abuse by family members can exile you from the entire concept and safety of family. Being exiled from a religious community because of your differences is another example. Being labeled as the black sheep of the family is being exiled from acceptance. All manner of hurtful experiences still come back to that same experience of being exiled from your sense of home and belonging, being severed from wholeness.

The art of working with your core wounds is the art of seeking wholeness while loving your brokenness. The pieces of yourself that were severed can find connection to the feeling of home again, even if you will always have the scars.

How do we see what these wounds are and tend to them? Through shadow work.

# What Is Shadow Work?

A lot of spirituality and healing practices revolve around the concept of *lightwork,* which focuses on personal growth through an intentionally positive lens. We need that positive lens. However, we exist in a world of contrast and balance. Our days are determined by how the light and the dark share existence, and our personal healing isn't exempt from these rules of shared existence. We are dark as much as we are light.

The concept of the *shadow archetype* was developed by famous Swiss psychiatrist and psychoanalyst Carl Jung. Jung described the shadow as "the unconscious aspect of the personality which the conscious ego does not identify in itself." It is the hidden parts of you, often encompassing your more "negative" aspects that you'd rather stay hidden to yourself and others. You can start recognizing what your shadow is by thinking of those automatic impulses you have to be unkind, to act in anger, to lie or steal or manipulate or run in fear. You can't fully understand or explain those impulses, you can only feel them beneath the surface and witness them popping up to cause chaos in your life. Shadow work is the process of confronting, understanding, and transforming those hidden aspects of yourself in order to heal and bring peace to your life.

Many avoid the shadow because they believe that by working with it, they are indulging the problems that grow and fester in darkness. What they fail to realize is that the festering is the very reason we must work with it. The shadow is the soil of your personal psychology. It not only determines what will grow in your life, but also determines *how* things will grow. Soil is integral to all growth, and we must each know our own soil to understand what grows from within. Those core wounds you have are the seeds planted in that soil a long time ago. They have taken root, no matter how much you wish it wasn't true. They are responsible for those darker impulses, and you must understand them to prevent them from causing chaos. Shadow work enables you to do that.

While lightwork focuses on the blooming plants reaching toward the warmth of the sun above, shadow work focuses on understanding and tending to the root system beneath the surface. It is tending to conditions for growth. For example, an exercise in lightwork would have you working on positive affirmations like "I am healed and connected to the divine" or "I am letting go of all that doesn't serve me." You recite them whenever you are feeling triggered as a way to focus on reaching for spiritual warmth. In contrast, an exercise in shadow work would have you figuring out *why* you don't feel healed and connected to the divine. You learn how to love your pain and your triggers and yourself enough to let go of what doesn't serve you. The lightwork affirmation doesn't account for the damage caused by your core wounding, whereas shadow work goes to the root of the damage. You can see that when shadow work and lightwork are used together in the proper way, beautiful progress can be made. But the shadow work aspect is often ignored in mainstream spirituality.

When you follow the spiritual journey of healing and lightwork, focused only on the positive lens, you inevitably reach a crossroads. This is the point where positive thinking has taken you forward a long way but cannot continue in good faith without the grounding influence of shadow work. If you veer left onto the path of shadow work, you can use your time in the shadow to address your persistent core wounds hidden deep inside you, and eventually loop it all together with the lightwork to create a powerful, authentic version of wholeness. This path offers a cohesive and deeply transformative experience, though it's not without challenges. This path of shadow work looks less manicured, less pretty, and more dangerous than the path of lightwork. It is harder to walk, as stumbling on stones and roots is guaranteed. Puddles on the path seem innocent but contain the depths of the ocean if you step into them. It is not necessarily a welcoming walk.

But if you instead veer right to stay on the same path of lightwork, you are crossing over into toxic positivity.

# Toxic Positivity

You can focus entirely on positive thinking while avoiding negative emotions. But dismissing and invalidating the authentic emotions involved creates imbalance. This is *toxic positivity*. If you dismiss your emotions long enough, you also cut off the ways to soothe and heal them. Without access to your true feelings, you inevitably cut off your access to growth. Continuing positive thinking with no access to growth only creates thought experiments that endlessly swirl in circles—without ever going anywhere useful. It feels good to think positively, but nothing shifts or changes as a result. Not only that, when used long enough, toxic positivity actually causes harm to the self and to others by dismissing your pain and the pain of others. It can trigger traumatic experiences and encourage dissociation from the mind and body.

No matter where you stand right now, whether you've hit the crossroads without veering into toxic positivity just yet, or you've unwittingly found yourself on that path already, there's no judgment here. In fact, I have great compassion for those who found themselves among toxic positivity, as I've been there myself. You can always choose differently now. You can always choose the other path. Choosing shadow work, choosing to embrace your emotions and work on your core wounds, will correct and heal the toxic positivity you've experienced.

# Shadowy Language

As you explore the shadow self and the realm of core wounds, you will find that there are thorny thickets and tender places everywhere. A word or a sentence you read may feel especially heavy to you or even rub you the wrong way. There's nothing wrong with this, as I would never ask you to simply overlook language that sits strangely with you. What I would ask, however, is that you approach the feelings with curiosity. *Why* does that word or sentence affect you? *Where* do the feelings come from? Those questions, and those moments you spend with yourself, are far more important than my ability to please every-one with every word. I do my best to explain what I mean in ways that bridge my understanding to yours, and each word I choose is fully intentional, with the weight of collective energy behind it. I find it's best not to attempt to sanitize my words. Instead, I trust your intelli-gence and experience to discern and extrapolate. Sit with me in this energy, and let's sort it out together.

# How to Use This Book

I recommend using a journal as you read the book, as there are prompts and exercises throughout the chapters. Your own reflections and your own process will make the work successful. You'll find that you may have moments of inspiration or remember things you'd forgotten, so it's important to log those moments while they're still fresh. Some people prefer to type out their experiences on a computer and others have even used a voice recorder to log their thoughts as an alternative to writing them down.

While the chapters are written in an intentional order, you may find that you are more drawn to certain chapters and certain exercises. Skipping over some exercises to work on others is okay, as that's likely a sign that there are parts of you bursting at the seams, ready for healing. Trust your intuition and what draws you. But also note what you are resistant to doing, as that holds power as well. Even if you skip parts, make sure to return to them so you can find out what waits for you there. I also recommend revisiting this book and these exercises multiple times throughout your healing journey, as your focus and your understanding will grow and change with every layer of work you do. Every time you revisit, you will relate to these different layers in varying ways.

## A Spiritual Approach

I like to make it very clear that I am not a therapist. Many of the themes and issues you'll work with in this book cross over into topics you may have worked with in therapy. In fact, many of my readers are therapists who recommend my books to their clients, and on the flip side, many of my readers bring these issues to their therapists to draw on an established support team. While this is true, I want to emphasize that I tackle these issues and themes from a spiritual and energetic approach first. My background is in spiritual healing work, and while I do work with clients in that capacity, this work does not run counter to the work you do with your behavioral health team. I encourage you to seek as much help and support as you need, in whatever form is most helpful to you.

## Following the Archetypes

These pages will take you on a journey through shadow work using archetypes to access and heal your core wounds. Using archetypes will help you conceptualize different aspects of your Shadow Self and different methods for creating pathways from your core wounds to the feeling of belonging that you yearn for. Think of your wholeness as a beautiful prism. Using archetypes is simply turning the prism in the sunlight, illuminating the different colors that shine from within. Each color offers a piece of the puzzle, a ray of light that's part of the rainbow.

You will open up the doors to the Shadow Self, creating an entirely new way to view your healing. You will tap into your intuition through the Higher Self, bring truth and acknowledgment to your core wounds through the Wounded Self, and learn how to gently reparent those wounds through the Compassionate Self. You will sort through the shadow of power dynamics and manipulation through the Powerful Self, learn how to work with your capacity through the Energetic Self, and embrace your natural instincts through the Primal Self. Armed with all this knowledge, you will channel your experiences through the Creative Self, and finally, be able to step into the wise neutrality of the Healed Self.

These archetypes will help you tend the system of your core wounds, creating feelings of peace and belonging in yourself. You don't have to feel guilty for having a Shadow Self. You don't have to feel like you will remain trapped in your trauma forever, doomed to repeat those patterns and cycles, again and again. Each time you learn how to give love and support to your wounds, you break the cycles and create new pathways from your shadow to your true home, your true wholeness.

Let's begin.

# CHAPTER 1

## • • • *The Shadow Self* • • •

My journey with shadow work started after I experienced some incredibly difficult and traumatic things. Things that broke me and made me lose my hope and faith in the world, in others, and in myself. Even after walking down the path of spirituality, experiencing the highs and the promises, I found that path wasn't enough. I didn't fit because I was too dark. I was always an outsider in one way or another, simply looking through the window into the light and love that others were experiencing, feeling only a slight dull warmth escaping through the corners of the windowpane and never the ultimate belonging they promised me. I found shadow work because I had to, because it was the only option available to me. My spirit was so full of energy, but the energy didn't have anywhere to go. It was considered negative or even a little dangerous to others on the path. Little did I know that shadow work was the path that would welcome all of that energy and all of me.

I come to you in these pages not as a guru or someone who would tell you what to do, but as someone who experienced what you have experienced, or maybe are experiencing right now in your life. I didn't have anyone to guide me through the intense portal of shadow work or tell me that my dark side not only had the potential to be negative and manipulative, but also to be powerful and wise when used in the right way. For the most part, I had to figure it out for myself, alone. So I'm here to help you feel more validated in your quest for the truth about yourself. To help you feel less alone. The things you will discover about yourself, and the way you are made up of both brilliantly bright stars that illuminate worlds and terrifying black holes that may destroy them, are the things that will unlock your true power and potential. Though your shadow may appear in scary or harmful ways, your shadow itself is not a threat. The way forward lies in how you recognize it and manage it. The most dangerous shadow is the one whose truth and origin is repressed. That also means that the most powerful shadow is the one whose truth and origin is dealt with and healed. It is now up to you to access your shadow and use it for truth and healing.

## The Hidden Parts of You

The Shadow Self is the first and most important archetype to get comfortable with. Your Shadow Self is the version of you that acts out based on the particular type of shadow you carry. Your shadow contains all the parts of you that are hidden from view, whether your own view or others' view. But your Shadow Self makes sure that those parts of you find the daylight through whatever means possible. This means that if you don't have a working relationship with your shadow, it is going to sneak around, sabotaging your efforts or creating chaos in your life. This is not done out of malice, but rather its desperate need for validation and self-expression.

Your Shadow Self doesn't only sabotage you, however. It is not made up of only the bad parts of yourself that are hidden, but also the good. Although we more often hide parts of us that may be perceived as bad, the shadow doesn't end there. Without regard for moral judgment, the shadow is made up of every part of you that is either unknown to you or others, or intentionally hidden from view. Keep this in mind, as even though I might define characteristics as "negative" or "positive" for simplicity's sake, that type of language implies moral judgment, which is not something your shadow is ruled by.

What your shadow is ruled by is truth. The shadow contains the most potent pieces of truth about yourself, the way you operate, and how you see the world. These truths include your experiences and feelings, your very nature. In this way, your shadow is not a portal of negativity, but a portal of truth. To get the most out of your shadow work journey, you must give yourself the grace and space to allow your perspective to shift. Relax your shoulders. Stop clenching your jaw. You don't need to fight yourself and your hidden aspects here. In shadow work, we welcome every part of you as an important piece of the truth of your wholeness. It's time to allow all of yourself to be involved in your healing.

## *Journal Prompts*

What is your current perception of what the Shadow Self is and is not?

What is your current perception of *your* Shadow Self?

How and why did you reach this point in your journey where you're ready to face your shadow?

To embark on this journey, what are some untrue beliefs about the shadow that you need to shift?

# Anatomy of a Wound

Even at the beginning of my spiritual journey, my need to address my core wounds was alive and well. I could already tell that my problems were connected to the deep and dark parts of me, the ones always just beneath the surface, waiting to be excavated. I was excited by the darkness somehow, like it was a mystery waiting to be solved, and I knew that spirituality would help me solve it. At the time, when all my spiritual communities and all the self-help books and classes repeatedly told me to ignore my urges to dive into the dark, I wondered what I was doing wrong. They insisted that speaking of wounded roots would only bring more negativity. So I went against my own instincts and tried it their way for a while, but my darkness kept seeping up through the soil of my soul and growing within me. Between fits of irritability and rage, triggered arguments with my loved ones, and a persistent state of dread, it was as if I could feel my Shadow Self trying to sabotage me in real time. The more often I requested others' permission to give attention to this unwelcome weed within, the more I was told to focus instead on positivity. Eventually, I had to break off from those communities and thought movements. My instincts were too strong, and though I didn't fully recognize it at the time, my intuitive self knew that the truth was being ignored. The feeling of being gaslit—being made to doubt my own reality—created such chaos inside me that I knew what I was being told was false.

Core wounds are seeds planted within us very early on in life. Regardless of circumstance, those seeds grow into something that lives inside of us and affects our very being and behavior. As they grow, they do sometimes feel and appear as if they are invasive weeds that need to be pulled and destroyed. Positive thinking might have you believing that as long as you only trim the leaves that are exposed on the outside, everything will be fine. You can imagine yourself without the weeds for positive results. You might also believe that the weed is your sin, your own personal root of evil and ego, and it must be destroyed at all costs to make room for the peaceful and perfect version of you. Both of these approaches neglect the beautiful and complicated ecosystem that is *you*.

Shadow work is not the art of cleaning up appearances so you're more palatable to the external world, nor is it the destruction of the thing that causes you pain. Shadow work is not beautification nor extermination. Shadow work is the art of gardening, tending the soil of your core wounds and understanding how the roots of everything are connected. It is a method of management. It is both compassion and tough love, balanced by discerning when to use which. The seeds of core wounds planted within you may have been invasive species, but guess what, after all these years, they *thrive* in your ecosystem. You cannot destroy them without compromising the very soil that makes up your spirit. You also cannot allow them to grow wild without tending, as they could overtake you and choke out all the other beautiful creations within you. The anatomy of those wounds make up the structure that helps you exist. This is why your worldview can shift so quickly when doing shadow work and healing, as the structure can move and change as if going through an earthquake. It is also why it is so very easy to lose yourself, your *real* self, when entering into spirituality, because when you are encouraged to destroy the very structure that helps you exist, you can easily fall away and disappear.

The good news (and bad news, depending on how you look at it) is that your shadow will never disappear forever. No matter how you try to change your structure, or root out the weeds within you, those original seeds will forever be growing. One way or another, you will have to deal with the wild bloom of your core wounds. You will have to learn how to garden, how to manage and hold the wisdom of your shadow in order to heal your core wounds.

This is also a good time to remind you about the nature of healing. I think it's important, especially when we're talking about core wounds, to remember that "healing" doesn't mean getting rid of or entirely curing a source of suffering. While there are times and circumstances when pain can be entirely cured, that is simply not the nature of psychology and core wounding. Healing is a spiral. As you heal, you move further and further along the spiral, constantly evolving and becoming a better version of yourself but not escaping the spiral altogether. You can also think of it as consistently addressing an issue, layer by layer, piece by piece. There are so many layers to healing, and it is unrealistic to think you can skip the delicate process of moving through the spiral or going through the many layers. We can make huge leaps, that is true, but we are never exempt from living in the spiral. Healing your core wounds means improving your life on the journey of the spiral, preventing those wounds from creating harm, improving your relationship with others and yourself, and finding a sense of peace and home.

# Manifestations of the Shadow

When I was told to repress my darker instincts, my shadow, it still found ways to come to the surface. That is simply the nature of core wounds. If you do not deal with them intentionally, you will still be forced to deal with them in other ways. Those ways are often more destructive and chaotic. For example, if you have a core wound of being abandoned, you may act on that wound by pushing people away and breaking ties before they can do it to you. If you are not dealing with that wound, you are actively destroying relationships and losing people while still experiencing that feeling of abandonment. You may unconsciously follow this pattern for years, losing so much time and love, always ending up alone and abandoned anyway. However, if you choose to engage that wound and work with it in a productive and protected way, you will avoid burning your life down while you heal. You'll end up feeling closer and more supported in your relationships as a result. Which way sounds better?

In order to make that choice, you need to recognize the manifestations of your shadow. Otherwise, you will act in ways that reinforce the nature and pain of the wound, so it continues growing, feral and unchecked. Here are some common manifestations of the shadow:

- Self-sabotaging relationships or opportunities
- Consciously or unconsciously triggering the pain points of others, or getting them to trigger your own
- Acting out (whatever that means to you)
- Holding anxiety and tension in your body
- Difficulty sleeping or sleeping too much
- Inability to follow healthy physical routines like hydration, nutrition, movement
- Feeling a compulsion to manipulate others, whether for personal gain or personal safety
- Finding yourself in the same bad situations over and over again, or with the same kind of person again and again
- Self-medicating with alcohol and substances
- Inability to say sorry or take responsibility for your actions
- Finding yourself in cycles of idealization and then demonization
- Chronic pain and fatigue
- Overreacting to others or becoming triggered very easily
- Mood swings and irritability
- Projecting your exact shadow onto others
- Feeling compelled to lie to or gaslight others for no real reason
- Avoiding your dreams and goals, as well as the things that make you happy

Shadow manifestations are often tangled with challenges like mental illness, addiction, generational trauma, and chronic illness. Shadow work does not override nor negate labeling and exploring those things with your appropriate support team. It only highlights the symptoms and consequences of your challenges, connecting them to your spiritual and psychological levels. Since shadow work looks at how many different pieces of ourselves come together, it should also be used in concert with other forms of support whenever necessary. Part of emotional and spiritual healing is knowing when to reach out to behavioral and medical professionals to create the most accurate picture of wholeness in yourself.

It may be hard to admit to doing some of the things on this list. No one wants to admit they are manipulating others or ending up in bad relationships time and time again. I want to remind you that there is no moral judgment in this part of the process. Having a shadow doesn't make you bad. Having certain patterns because of your core wounds doesn't make you a bad person. That's not how it works. Moralism is often a trap filled with contradictions that are meant to protect you from confronting your own shadow. It is a defense mechanism. If you see things as only being able to be bad or good, you are less likely to even step into the "bad" world.

Being a human is not a matter of being only bad or good though.

As you work on identifying and facing your negative, shadowy traits, keep in mind that no one is here to judge you. The truth is that we are all horribly flawed people. It's important to be honest with yourself, as you cannot heal what you cannot point out. Having a shadow, having trauma, is not a moral failing. Without flinching, I can tell you a few of my own shadow traits. Because of trauma, I can have both the automatic tendency to victimize myself or self-sabotage, and the compulsion to manipulate others as a learned survival tactic. I don't blame myself for having those shadowy aspects, as I understand the root of them and why they exist. I do trust myself to do inner work so those aspects don't unconsciously run my life or harm myself or others. But I do not judge myself. The only time judgment reasonably comes into play in shadow work is when you don't take responsibility for what your patterns and wounds create. By diving into these pages and doing the work, you are taking responsibility and claiming your power to create change within yourself and within the world.

Because the shadow is hidden and unconscious, you cannot expect to make its entirety seen and conscious in one attempt or by reading through this book once. You will reveal it layer by layer. By bringing light to these hidden traits of yourself over time, you are revealing the aspects of your shadow that will bring change and healing to your life when you are ready for it.

## *Journal Prompts*

How does your shadow manifest? Which behaviors on the list resonate with you?

Which manifestations are the hardest to admit, and why?

Seeing all of this, how do you think your core wounds and your shadow manifest in your relationships with others?

How do you think your core wounds and your shadow manifest in your relationship with yourself?

What is your experience with moral judgment and seeing things in black and white? Can you see where in your experience you might need to offer yourself more grace?

# Talents Tangled Up in Trauma

The shadow is made up of what is hidden, so it must also be true that your shadow also contains the wonderful and creative parts of you that have gone unnoticed or unexplored. Carl Jung described the shadow as "the seat of creativity," housing both the unconscious negative aspects *and* the unconscious positive aspects. This becomes obvious when we consider some of the positive skills and talents we have that can only be uncovered when we deal with our unconscious negative aspects. For example, perhaps you were a very creative child with a talent for artistic expression. Maybe your core wounds, the seeds of your trauma, originated in a way that made you feel you were no longer allowed to express yourself artistically, so you gave it up. If you have trauma surrounding your long-buried gift, there's no way to access it now unless you are brave enough to enter into the trauma of the shadow as well. While you may be avoiding the pain of your shadow because you think it's easier, you may also be avoiding the joy and creativity of your brilliant self at the same time—which inevitably makes everything harder. There is so much power hidden within that's woven into the more difficult parts of the shadow. It's your job to reclaim that power.

Kate had a gift for music and songwriting in her teen years. She went through some really traumatic experiences during that timeframe and used music as her solace, her coping mechanism. She even went so far as to say that having an outlet for her truth saved her life at the time. As she got older, even though she worked with her trauma for years, she played music less and less. As an adult, she excused this loss as "part of growing up and being a boring adult." But then one day Kate went to a music store with a friend. As she looked at the rows of guitars and touched the smooth blond wood on one that looked like her old guitar, emotion swelled and she struggled against the tears in her eyes. In that moment, touching that guitar, her real pain came through.

"I don't deserve it," she whispered quietly. Kate realized how much of her trauma was tied up in her lost passion for music. In her trauma, she was made to believe that she was worthless and didn't deserve good things in her life. She was made to believe that she was abused because she deserved abuse. Because her lifeline was music, those false beliefs about her worth inevitably became warped and twisted into that lifeline. For Kate, approaching music again was a significant part of her healing. We worked on this together in baby steps, and every step she took opened the floodgates of stuck trauma and emotion. It was painful and hard, but each step took her closer to the creative, talented self trapped inside, hidden in the shadow. The more she worked through the wounding and came back to her gift, the more alive and whole she felt, like she was herself again, playing her music.

Eliza grew up in a home full of anger. Both her parents displayed bouts of rage that seemingly came out of nowhere. If she was in the wrong place at the wrong time, her parents' anger was unfairly directed at her, whether through screaming, criticizing, or even physical abuse. As a result, Eliza learned how to read her parents closely. She developed the survival skill of keen observation as she walked on eggshells, watching her parents for any signs that they were about to go off. Because she knew the signs, she was often able to defuse the situation or leave it entirely before her parents exploded. As an adult, however, Eliza found herself in bad company and situations, time and time again. She couldn't seem to be able to read the red flags in any given situation. As we worked on her wounding, she discovered that even though she possessed the incredible ability to read people accurately, she intentionally pushed it away because it reminded her of the trauma. But pushing away the trauma also pushed away the skill, which then affected her life negatively. Eliza's healing involved recovering her discernment without drowning in the trauma. Once she was able to use her discernment in a positive way in her life, healthier relationships developed almost immediately.

Like Kate and Eliza, we all have amazing gifts and power hidden in our shadow. Being able to identify your shadow traits is the art of bringing what is hidden into the light. It may be easier to identify your more negative shadow aspects, as you did in the previous section, because they seem more obvious. But if you remember that nothing is black and white, bad and good, and that power and joy are always tangled up in the trauma, you will discover the doors that also lead you back to your most embodied self.

## *Journal Prompts*

Think back to some of the talents or hobbies you enjoyed that got tangled up in trauma. What were those hobbies and what happened?

How are your relationships to those talents and hobbies now?

How do you think your experiences of life and yourself would change if some of those things came back into your life?

What are some of the things you are particularly skilled at *because* of your wounding?

# Seedy Underbellies

Focusing only on ourselves can cause us to lose perspective as we explore the shadow. So it is helpful to zoom out and see that not only individual humans have shadow sides. Everything that contains structure contains shadow. Civilizations, governments, the seasons of nature, animals, philosophies. Realizing this builds your critical thinking and observational skills in a world that desperately needs them. It also builds your personal intuition and emotional intelligence to think in this way.

Every creature, every structure, has an underbelly. It is hidden and where we are vulnerable. The phrase "seedy underbelly" describes the dark and corrupt side of things. When a cat exposes their underbelly to you, displaying a certain level of trust, it's considered a high compliment. The underbelly is not just where our corruptions lie, but where our vulnerabilities lie too. Both of those things reveal context and priceless gems of truth that make our lives more interesting and beautiful when used correctly. It's certainly easier to identify corruptions and vulnerabilities in the shadows of external structures and systems, but remember that your own shadow will be touched or even defined by those very structures as well.

Practice seeing the macrocosm of the collective and bringing it into the microcosm of your individual healing. This quick, meaningful shift between perspectives makes a huge impact in everything you do. Try watching the news and noticing how current events trigger certain feelings deep within you. How do those events and those feelings reflect back the seedy underbelly of the world, and in turn, your own shadowy vulnerabilities? We are creatures of our collective environment. The root systems of our core wounds are all connected in one huge root system below.

Remember when I wrote that moralism is often a trap designed to keep you from facing or confronting anything labeled "bad"? External systems and hierarchies that use strictly bad versus good mindsets almost always benefit from you avoiding what they deem to be bad. Keep in mind that your own personal moral compass and the weaponization of morals are two separate things. The hierarchies focused on weaponizing morals do so in order to control you within the sector of "good" behavior while preventing you from noticing the "bad" behavior they are engaged in. Those systems will cease to have power over you if you are actively engaging with the bad and creating change. As you work with your shadow, remember that it is steeped in the shadow of these systems as well. This brings another complicated layer of context that emphasizes the need for neutrality and compassion when it comes to moral judgment.

## *Journal Prompts*

Where do you see the shadow in the external world? What structures and systems make the shadow seem obvious to you?

How do those shadowy systems reflect back on your own shadow and wounding? How are you affected by them? Did those systems help create your wounds?

Where do you see moralism from others as they try to control you or interfere with your own moral compass?

# Shadow Work and Positive Thinking

Shadow work and positive thinking have a very tenuous relationship. They are very different, even appearing as opposites at times, but they also need one another. The most common example of this conflict is how positive thinking often stays positive by pushing away or denying all negativity and shadowy aspects. In that context, the positive thought is not positive in spite of, or in relationship to, the shadow. It is positive only by taking the shadow out of the equation entirely, dumping it into the "negative vibes" category and refusing to acknowledge it. This creates an alarmingly simple division of truth that is based on denial. By taking "negative vibes" out of the equation and zeroing in on "good vibes only," those good vibes run the risk of becoming dogmatic and based in fantasy rather than truth. Are the vibes only good because you've integrated the shadow and are meaningfully creating change alongside it? Or are they only good because you're simply ignoring the existence of the bad?

This is where *spiritual bypassing* comes in. Spiritual bypassing is the act of denying or ignoring very real experiences of pain and suffering, both in yourself and in others. It encourages maintaining an idyllic version of spirituality instead, one where pain and victimhood no longer exist, one that doesn't truly exist in the world. This is where positive thinking turns into toxic positivity. Others may impose this on you and also encourage you to impose it on yourself and others. Spiritual bypassing is more common in groups who experience more economic and racial privilege than marginalized groups. They are quick to dismiss someone's negative experiences or worldviews in favor of platitudes of oneness that lack grounding in the real world. This is the person who tells you that you're in economic hardship because you create your own reality and you've created a negative one for yourself, without considering the very real systemic barriers that contribute to poverty. Or they say that you experienced an abusive relationship because you "called in" that particular abuse due to your lack of spiritual fortitude and need for perspective, without considering the impact of childhood trauma and the abuse cycle.

Yes, all spiritual tokens and sayings contain grains of truth. You *do* have a lot of power in your life to create new circumstances. You can change your relationship to your boundaries and experience different kinds of people. You can end terrible patterns and cycles. All these things are true, but you need to engage your shadow in order to do it. To gloss over the very real existence of barriers like trauma, cultural disparity, racial discrimination, and class inequity indicates a lack of compassion, awareness, and knowledge of basic history.

Instead of zooming in on cultural and psychological factors, toxic positivity pushes away history and fact in favor of delusion. A *delusion* is a false belief about external reality. While it has specific connotations in behavioral health, the broader definition is important in this context. Delusions about reality formed by toxic positivity inherently blame the victim and prosper in privilege. They include beliefs that everything will always be okay, that everyone can create their own reality, that all you need to do is focus on what you want to manifest, and the rest doesn't matter. Toxic positivity relies on those delusions and requires that you also believe "the rest doesn't matter." In this context, "the rest" is history and income inequality and racism and misogyny and political injustice and all manner of human-created pain. History is filled with horrors against humanity and the planet. The truth of it feels awful. It hurts. Delusion, on the other hand, feels good. Delusion doesn't create friction or pain. Delusion is a vacation from history, so why *wouldn't* you want that?

Spiritual bypassing has a very specific function. It's designed to allow a person to stay in delusion, on vacation from history, and retain that sense of gained peace, even when that peace was falsely found. Shadow work acknowledges history. It understands that history reveals origins (including your core wounds), motivations, and patterns that continue into the future. If you are unaware of history and the shadowy origin of it, you cannot truly break the patterns and create the ripples of joy and healing that you crave.

The shadowy part of systems and civilizations oppress and take advantage of people. They rely on you to bypass history and stay in your bubble of delusion. If you are in delusion and don't see what's wrong, why would anything change? They benefit from a faulty cultural memory, because if you are not remembering the origin of the wound, they can continue wounding you and reaping the rewards without worrying about you dismantling or changing the system. Many people even claim history is boring, which I believe is a short-sighted and pointed way to encourage you to avoid the truth of it. It is not until you know the shadow, with its history and its manipulation tactics, that you can change the system. Let's be honest—the system *needs* to be changed. Whether we're talking about the larger external system or the complex system within you and your own personal history, it needs healing.

On the flip side of this deep exploration, when you become immersed in shadow work or studying the historical truth of things, it can be easy to become jaded and lose hope. This is where shadow work does need positive thinking. Not spiritual bypassing, not ignoring or denying that a problem exists, and not delusion, but brave and bare-faced hope in the face of and alongside the shadow. Positive thinking in its greatest form acknowledges and appreciates the pain of humanity, while leaving space for what is beautiful. It is the lotus growing from the mud, the dandelion blooming in the crack of the concrete. Allowing yourself to use positive thinking without letting it creep across the line into toxic positivity will give your shadow work journey staying power and incentive.

## *Journal Prompts*

How have you experienced spiritual bypassing and toxic positivity from others? How have they affected your relationship with yourself and the world?

Which life experiences of yours did positive thinking try to override or ignore?

How have you tried to spiritually bypass yourself in your healing journey?

What are some things in your life that you've been intentionally delusional about, as a way to protect yourself from the truth?

What is your relationship to history? (This could mean global history, family history, history of yourself, and more.)

How has ignoring history benefited you in the short term? How has it hurt you in the long term?

# In the Gap Between Reality and Fantasy

Toxic positivity can be commonly found in teachings on positive affirmations and manifestation. These positive short phrases or beliefs are meant to help you achieve amazing results. Before you start shaking your head at me, let's get this out of the way: Sometimes they work. Sometimes they help. In fact, I often use positive affirmations when working on healing and doing ritual work. Remember, there is no absolute here. But context matters.

The major pitfall is that teachers of positive affirmations and manifestation do not acknowledge shadow and core wounding. You are encouraged to write "I am powerful and nothing can hurt me!" on a Post-it note, as if sticking it on your mirror and reading it every morning will magically change everything. At the same time, no one asks you *why you don't feel powerful* and *how you were hurt*.

If you are told to override your negative experiences in favor of manifesting this positive affirmation, you are creating a gap between reality and fantasy without leaving room for honesty. The further the gap widens, the more cognitive dissonance will be created, which means you certainly won't achieve your goal or find lasting healing. If you can't be honest about the place you're starting from, how can you ever expect to bridge the gap and know where you're going?

Take, for example, someone who wants to manifest their soulmate. Using positive affirmations and manifestation, they will be solely focused on the joy and success of finding that one special person for them. But what if they have a history of relationship abuse? What if they have a demonstrated lack of boundaries and the inability to discern their own needs from others' needs as a result of that trauma? Any soulmate they might actually attract will be unable to give them the relationship they desire with all their shadow baggage. Or worse, they may attract another abusive partner without seeing the red flags because of those wounds. Neither person will be able to love or be loved fully. Not without working on their core wounds, breaking their patterns and cycles, and establishing loving boundaries first.

Another easy example is someone trying to manifest wealth. If their financial reality is filled with a lot of debt and an inability to create or follow a budget, no amount of reading "I am a millionaire!" on their bathroom mirror will help change that. Alternatively, they could seek the origin of their inability to budget (often a shadow manifestation connected to feeling powerless, by the way) and then take small steps to change their reality. If they also address their shadow relationship with money and power, then their positive affirmation will feel closer to the truth and more attainable. Even changing their affirmation to something gentler and more realistic would be helpful, so instead of "I am a millionaire!" it may instead be "I am making and saving more every month!" As a side note, keep in mind that everything you want to manifest involving wealth and power is also attached to those pesky cultural and systemic shadows, which adds more spicy ingredients to the recipe.

Positive affirmations, when applied alongside shadow work and the acknowledgment of history and core wounding, will help bridge that gap between reality and fantasy. Acknowledging your wounds, the *whys* and *hows* behind your affirmations, creates a grounded and honest starting point in your journey. The less cognitive dissonance, the better. Whatever steps you take, however big or small, need to be both sustainable and grounded in the reality of wherever you're standing right now. If you can put in this work, you'll find that your affirmations and manifestations have a much better success rate.

# Everything Is Medicine in the Correct Dosage

Nothing is black and white, especially when it comes to the individual spiritual and emotional journey. There are too many variables, and context is needed to fully understand what's in front of us. Keep that in mind when approaching your relationship to both shadow work and positive thinking.

As I point out the pitfalls of positive thinking and why it hasn't fulfilled its promises to you, I also want to remind you that positive thinking isn't inherently bad, in the same way that the shadow isn't inherently bad. It's all about how you apply it. In the right moments, in the right situations, positive thinking is exactly what is needed to inject hope and comfort. It can keep encouraging you to put one foot in front of the other. But let's say you keep encountering the same trauma triggers in the world or the same toxic arguments with your partner. In those cases, where you keep coming up against a repeating pattern, saying something positive to change the subject and move on is one of the worst things you could do. Not only does that ignore the context of the trigger or negative feeling, but it forces you to lie to others and yourself about your feeling's very existence. It widens that gap between fantasy and reality and brings you right back to toxic positivity.

The same goes for shadow work itself. If you are so immersed in the traumatic history of your wounding that you are unable to enjoy the pleasures in life—the joy and beauty that the world can offer—it is no longer a potent medicine, but a poison. You must use everything in the correct dosages. When it comes to shadow work, the antidote is the poison, applied differently. It's like the well-known nightshade Belladonna, famous for its ability as a fatal poison in large doses. But used in small doses in the correct context, Belladonna is a medicinal treatment for insomnia, colic, and ulcers. The results completely change with intention, context, and dosage. Belladonna may be an extreme example, but it applies to almost everything. Even delicious sugary desserts, eaten as an occasional treat, are harmless and delightful. But too much, too often makes you sick and has negative effects on your health. Your discernment is especially important here, as you are the only one with the power to fully recognize how and when to shift your dosages.

# Selves of the Shadow

Now that you have a better understanding and appreciation of your Shadow Self, you're ready to engage the healing process with awareness and validation. As you go through the following chapters, you'll be able to apply the concepts and exercises to your shadow, noticing the ways your Shadow Self shows itself. Each Self archetype that you'll learn about represents various mythical parts of your being that can help you understand and integrate your Shadow Self. But none of them are separate from the shadow. I want you to get used to the idea that your Shadow Self is in everything, every part of you. You cannot escape the influence of your shadow, even if you've tried in vain to hide it. Each Self archetype has the blood of your shadow running through it and giving it life with every heartbeat. By working alongside your shadow as a friend, rather than against it as an enemy, you will bring so much rich and meaningful healing to your core wounds and to your life.

# CHAPTER 2

### • • • *The Higher Self* • • •

My Higher Self often appears to me as a combination of mist and wind. She moves with the breeze, as a mystical version of someone might. She knows all about my past and my trauma, and she has more than enough love and wisdom to offer as I continually venture to heal. Sometimes, I hear her voice through the wind in the trees. She is the one who connects me to my intuition and the Universe, which shows up in fascinating ways. I often dream about animals, as I have always loved nature and can feel their individual messages and meanings. My Higher Self helps me understand them. Sometimes, I hear a loud ringing in my ear, which is a "Yes!" when I'm debating a choice or decision. I often feel her influence as I am doing a healing session on a client. She's in the sensations in my body, the inner sense of knowing, the heat and the sparkles and the brief images that come as useful metaphors for my client—all flowing with ease when I connect to my Higher Self as I work. At times, she haunts me with her endless knowing of my pain, her limitless compassion for my struggle. At other times, she inspires me with her levity and her ease. She is a part of me, she *is* me, and she is also separate from me. All in all, I wouldn't be able to do what I do without her. I wouldn't be able to handle my core wounds and integrate my shadow without her, let alone help anyone else do the same.

What's the best part about working with my Higher Self? She reminds me that whoever I'm working with also has their own Higher

Self, and their Higher Self will always know what is best for them. She reminds me that my only real job is to help the other person communicate better with themselves. And that's why you're here.

# Exalted, Connected, and Wise

The Higher Self is the exalted aspect of you. It is your spiritual self, the part of you that is connected to the divine. It is the wisest and most enlightened version of you. Keep in mind that "divine" can mean anything to you, as it's not connected to a particular religion or belief. It's simply the part of you that's connected to the collective unconscious of the world, the higher intelligence of nature and the Universe. Your Higher Self can give you guidance on living your life in the truest and most aligned way for you.

Some may confuse the Higher Self as being the opposite of the Shadow Self, in the way that light is the opposite of darkness. However, in the same way that some may perceive the Shadow Self as the bad part of you, the flawed human version, they may then perceive the Higher Self as the good part of you, the perfected spiritual version. It may be an easy automatic assumption to make, but it is much more nuanced. The Higher Self and the Shadow Self are complimentary in nature, and each needs the other in order to develop and grow. They are more interlinked than they are opposites. You cannot access the true gifts of your Higher Self without intimately knowing your Shadow Self, and you cannot even begin to traverse the depths of your Shadow Self without the guidance of your Higher Self. Your Higher Self will be able to give you important answers when working with your core wounds, but the information needs to go through your Shadow Self as well.

The Higher Self is also needed on this part of the journey because as it encourages you to trust your deepest instincts, it also brings much needed joy and fun to a process that can feel overwhelmingly heavy.

While bringing the keys you need to unlock the doors to your core wounds, it often does so in a way that inspires personal meaning and connection.

How do you establish and grow this relationship to your Higher Self? You embolden your intuition.

## *Journal Prompts*

Describe your Higher Self as you know them right now.

What is your relationship to your Higher Self and how do they communicate with you?

# The Chakra System

While it's likely that you've come across the chakra system in your healing already, this is a good time to revisit it, as it can be an incredibly helpful tool to develop your intuition and open channels of communication with your Higher Self. The word "chakra" translates to "wheel" in Sanskrit, and there are seven primary chakras, or wheels of energy, that travel up your spine. Each chakra is its own energy center, and represents and influences different physical, emotional, and spiritual aspects of your being. The root chakra, at the base of your spine, is represented by the color red and pertains to physical survival, stability, and grounding. The sacral chakra, just below the bellybutton, is the color orange and represents creativity, sexuality, emotions, and self-worth. The solar plexus chakra, in the upper abdomen, is yellow and represents willpower, confidence, and self-esteem. The heart chakra, in the center of the chest, is green and represents love, compassion, and forgiveness. The throat chakra is blue and represents communication and truth. The third eye, in the center of the forehead, is indigo and represents intuition and imagination. The crown, at the top of the head in violet, represents intelligence and your connection to the divine.

Having chakras that are energetically too open or too closed can create imbalances not only in your spiritual life but also your emotional and physical life. Meditating with the chakras is a great way to strengthen your intuition and connect your Higher Self to your body in a way that promotes healing, giving you more information on your core wounds. For example, many empaths have blockages and imbalances in their sacral chakra, as that area holds emotion. Meditating on their sacral chakras using orange-toned visualizations as an aid can release some of the stuck emotional energy. This creates a release, oftentimes flooding the mind with visuals or intuitive information on their core wounding around emotions.

In simplified terms for our uses in this book, the lower chakras govern the physical body and its connection to the earth. The higher chakras govern the spirit body and its connection to the divine. The divide is usually at the heart chakra, which functions as the gateway. The heart chakra is often where our overall blocked energy is. You must keep that flow of energy open between the lower chakras and the higher chakras to heal, create, and regulate.

As you experiment with chakra meditation or work with an energy healer, take notes on what you're drawn to, how you feel about the colors, and what comes up as you approach each chakra. Start developing a sense of which of your core wounds sit in which chakras, and how they manifest emotionally and physically. Notice where the flow of energy from your root chakra to your crown chakra is impeded or feels overloaded. Having a system that helps organize this intuitive information is an incredibly helpful tool, as the Higher Self and the body can sometimes feel at odds.

# The Higher Self and the Body

The primary difference between your Higher Self and the rest of you is that the Higher Self works much quicker and on different levels than your Shadow Self and your physical body. Because of this, it often appears and manifests quite differently as well. Your Higher Self is directly connected to a wealth of knowledge and wisdom that transcends time and space. The divine part of you isn't beholden to the physical laws of the earth and the body. This is why you can intuitively have information drop into your consciousness with no warning, or why you can understand something in your mind long before your physical body can integrate it or use it. This can become a problem when you realize that your physical body is being slowed down by dense energies, blockages, and simple physical drives like hunger and tiredness. For this reason, your body will always be playing catch-up with your spirit.

While this may seem like a design flaw in the system, it's a necessary reminder to stay connected to your body and its needs. Being a human on this planet is *not* an easy feat. You are existing in pure physical form and pure spiritual form all at once, and you must create a bridge from one to the other in order to keep sane and healthy.

Because our core wounds are the seeds of our trauma, and we know that trauma lives in the body as much as the mind, we need to able to address the body and mind simultaneously in order to find healing. Too much focus on developing the Higher Self without tending to the body with the same amount of care can cause all sorts of issues, including dissociation, anxiety, and even spiritual madness. This is when you are overloading energy in your higher chakras, like your crown and third eye, while your lower chakras, like the root and sacral, are disconnected, blocked, or ungrounded. Think of overloaded higher chakras like a lightbulb with too much wattage and no grounding line. The light itself isn't the problem, the flow of it is. Not only can this overload break the precious lightbulb, it separates the above and the below. That kind of separation also leads you on the path of toxic positivity, as it pulls you out of the physical reality you live in and drains you of the perspective and humanity of the physical world.

The opposite problem happens as well, when you are so immersed and overwhelmed by your daily physical life and all its stressors that you are not tending to your Higher Self. In this case, you have energetic imbalances in your lower chakras without using your higher chakras to connect and balance you. This can lead to problems like depression, lack of purpose and inspiration, and an overall feeling of disconnection from intuitive knowledge and divinity. Only through the balanced, healthy flow of energy between the physical body and the Higher Self, between the lower chakras and the higher chakras, can we heal core wounds. This means that you need to be in tune with both the needs of your Higher Self and your body.

Your body needs more time and more tools for integration. One way you can give your body what it needs is to nurture its basic needs as much as you can. Hydration, sleep, nutrition, supplementation, necessary medicine, and movement are all incredibly important—especially when working through the kind of energy you experience when healing your core wounds. Any kind of physical self-care is helpful when your body is playing catch-up with the work your spirit is doing.

Your Higher Self, on the other hand, needs a clear pathway to express itself. Energetic blockages within you will make it harder for you to understand what your Higher Self is trying to communicate to you. A meditative clearing practice is key here, as it both develops skills for working with your intuition and turns your attention to creating as clear a path as possible for that important information. It's also important to tend to your mental health as part of this care, through whatever form of support works for you.

## *Journal Prompts*

Do you find that you lean more toward too much focus on your Higher Self, or too much focus on your physical body? How so?

In what ways does your daily life interfere with your ability to connect to your Higher Self?

In what ways does your quest for your Higher Self neglect your body's needs?

What can you specifically do to support your physical body's needs for integration and adjustment?

What can you specifically do to support your Higher Self's needs for expression?

# Intuition and the "Clairs"

There are many ways to connect to your Higher Self and your intuition, and the easiest way to begin is by exploring the *clairs*—the intuitive abilities connected to the senses. The four most widely known clairs include clairvoyance, clairsentience, clairaudience, and claircognizance.

Clairvoyance is the most known on the list and is connected to the sense of sight, or clear seeing. This means that if you're more likely to experience visions and images, or maybe even see movies in your mind, your sense of clairvoyance is strong. You may also see auras or colors around people or animals, and you may be able to see ghosts or spirits.

Psychic dreams also fit into this category.

Clairsentience is connected to the sense of feeling and touch, or clear feeling. This is the primary clair for many empaths and sensitives, as they are likely to feel someone else's energy in their own mind and body. This could mean feeling tingles or pain in connection to someone else or yourself, or even being able to feel the energy in a room when you walk in.

Clairaudience is connected to the sense of hearing, or clear hearing. This can mean hearing actual sounds and messages, or feeling as though a message has simply dropped into your mind out of nowhere. It can include hearing a buzzing or ringing in your ears or experiencing a lot of energy and power in music.

Claircognizance is connected to the sense of knowing, or clear knowing. This is the most direct of all the clairs, as it happens when you get an immediate download from your intuition. You just "know" it, even if you can't explain how it came to you.

There are other lesser experienced clairs, including clairsalience (clear smelling), clairgustance (clear tasting), clairtangency (clear touching), and clairempathy (or clear emotion).

Connecting with your naturally dominant clairs and developing your less dominant ones will help to create a clearer pathway between you and your Higher Self. If you know how your Higher Self likes to communicate, do everything in your ability to make it as easy as possible. Don't think of it like you are developing some mystical skill you don't have; instead, look at it like you already have an innate mastery of your intuition. You only need to discover the correct pathway it likes to take and then keep that flow clear and open.

Knowing how to do this will make the difficult shadow work journey easier and will help heal trauma and the manifestations of your core wounds. How? Let me give you some examples.

Tina's natural gift was clairsentience. She could feel pains and tingles in her body that weren't connected to actual physical pains, but never knew what they meant. In her shadow work journey, she knew she had a lot of trauma trapped in her cells from a history of domestic violence and also some old injuries in her pelvic area. When we worked together and used a method of somatic healing, I guided her to identify where pockets of trauma lived in her body. With her gift of feeling, she became adept at quickly identifying where her trauma was. She could feel heaviness and pain in different places, and when we explored that area together, she was able to more effectively release the trapped emotions there. Because of her gift, she was also able to tell when she was successful at releasing, as it gave her tingles and a new sense of openness in her body.

Joel had a gift for clairaudience. He was a musician and was already very sensitive to sound and audio. In fact, he also had sensory issues around sound, as too much sound at once was overstimulating. He listened to different frequencies and soundwaves individually, meditating on them as a way to clear his intuitive channels and hear more. This practice allowed him to experience more messages dropping into his mind as if his brain was already playing a song stuck in his head. These messages were helpful pieces of information about how he could integrate his shadow. They were messages from his inner child, helping him pinpoint the roots of his core wounds. Being able to access this information made the healing process easier for him, and he often experienced synchronicity with the music he was listening to.

Erin had a talent for claircognizance. She would often describe a feeling of "just knowing" something rather than having a sensory experience of it first. It came across in both simple things, like knowing which song was going to come on next on the radio, to bigger things, like knowing someone's specific problems before being told. Because she had no reason to know these things, she would doubt herself and brush off her instincts, sometimes even going against what she knew in rebellion. She also found that others wouldn't take her knowing seriously, which made her doubt herself even more. As we worked on her core wounds together, we found that her first instincts would always be on target, but she would immediately turn away from them. One of her core wounds was that she wasn't believed as a child, so her core wound was acting itself out on her very intuition, creating storms of self-sabotage in anticipation of rejection from others. It wasn't until she was able to trust her own instincts that she was also able to approach her core wounds, as they were inextricably linked. The more she developed this relationship, the faster her life began to tangibly improve. She was able to leave or avoid circumstances not meant for her and know quickly which direction she wanted to take instead.

Figuring out how your Higher Self and intuition wants to speak to you will make your healing journey that much smoother and more meaningful. Try the following exercises to work on your unique connections to the clairs.

## *EXERCISE:* EXPERIMENTING WITH THE CLAIRS

These easy exercises get you started on experiencing the different clairs and figuring out which ones feel the most natural for you. Continuous practice will strengthen your abilities.

*Clairvoyance:* Try focusing on an object or even a person in front of you. Work on breathing deeply and steadily as you allow your gaze to soften. Set your intention for your third eye chakra to open. As you breathe and soften, you may begin to notice little flashes, sparks, colors, or a glow around various objects or people. This may take some time, so keep coming back to this practice. As you're gazing, you can also begin to ask yourself questions, like "What do I need for my healing?" Your intuition may put images in your mind or even in your visual environment.

*Clairsentience:* Focus on breathing slowly and set your intentions. Rub your hands together for a few moments. Then use your hands to slowly scan over your body (or you can also do this with a friend). As you scan, notice any sensations you feel in your hands or in your body. Most likely, it will be tingling or feelings of heat or cold. As you move your hands, notice when the sensations change and where in your body you feel the most energy. You can also experiment by moving your hands to create a ball of energy between them, and once you feel the energetic form of it, you can use your intention to make that ball of energy bigger and bigger so you can extend your hands while still feeling the tingling form of the energy.

*Clairaudience:* Get yourself into a meditative state where your breathing is steady and your intentions are set. Now try intoning by chanting a singular note or sound. As you make this tone, let the sound expand in your ears, experimenting with raising and lowering your volume. Continue this process for at least a few minutes. As you do this, you may notice a specific ringing in your ear, or you may even hear multiple notes in the one note you're toning. Pay attention to whether you are getting messages dropped into your mind, like a song stuck in your head.

*Claircognizance:* Because claircognizance is inner knowing without provocation, this form of intuition is strengthened through trust. This is where you are making conscious decisions to trust your instincts without knowing why. You can do this in incredibly simple ways, like going down a particular aisle to find a parking spot, or choosing what to wear for the day, or selecting a movie to watch. If you can build your senses using small things, you'll be able to trust yourself enough to rely on it when making bigger decisions, like whether you should accept that job or not, whether you need to leave your relationship, or whether a person or situation is worth your energy and investment.

# Synchronicity as a Map

How will you know if you're on the right track when developing your relationship to your Higher Self? Synchronicity is always a fun and reliable way to track your progress. Synchronicity is the phenomenon of multiple occurrences happening simultaneously in a way that inspires meaningful coincidence for those experiencing it. Synchronicity can appear in many ways, and it's often your Higher Self leaving you clues. It can include seeing repeating symbols or messages in the world and in nature, like noticing the same numbers over and over again or seeing the same animal. It can be when you are thinking of a friend and they text you in the same moment. It could be dreaming of a specific item that you see in real life the next day. Anything that stands out as a meaningful coincidence can be synchronicity guiding you to something important or validating something you're feeling or doing. It may even be the case that you're reading this book because of some level of synchronicity—maybe your friend told you about shadow work and you saw this book randomly the same afternoon. Synchronicity is especially important as a tool when you haven't quite figured out the best or clearest ways to communicate with your Higher Self, because it puts little arrows and directions right in your path in the most obvious ways.

I'm going to share a story about the breadcrumbs of synchronicity. The details may seem mundane and unimportant, but just go with me and see how it all eventually connects. Lena got brunch with her friend. Though she was a coffee lover, she declined coffee that day, as her digestive system had been off for a while and she didn't know why. She talked to her friend about her romantic relationship. Lena had been considering ending it for months, but couldn't figure out whether it was the right thing to do. There was a lot of anger and resentment she held back in the relationship, in fear of rocking the boat. Her friend tried to comfort Lena and suggested they go horseback riding together, as it was one of her favorite hobbies and Lena had never tried it. Lena shrugged it off. After lunch, Lena stopped at a thrift store and bought a yellow sweater she normally wouldn't have chosen. For some reason, the cheerful color was calling her name. Next to the sweater she purchased, she noticed a shirt with a horse on it. When she looked at the bulletin board full of business cards on her way out of the building, Lena noticed a card for an energy healer offering an introductory deal. She had always been curious, and she was feeling a little desperate in her romantic situation, so she called the healer and scheduled a session for a few days later. That night, Lena dreamed she was riding a horse on the beach. But as she was riding, in addition to holding the reins, her arms were filled with random objects and she kept losing them. She was filled with anxiety over losing the objects. On the day of the session, the energy healer told Lena that she had a major blockage in her solar plexus chakra. The color of this chakra is yellow. There was an issue with her sense of willpower about making a decision, and the healer also said that the blockage there could cause issues with digestion and detox. That chakra houses the liver, which represents unexpressed anger.

Lena was blown away by all the little dots connecting—the repressed anger, the digestion, the color yellow, the sweater she'd purchased. At the end of the session, the healer recommended a few options for her to try next. One of her suggestions was working with horses. With all the synchronicity, Lena did try riding horses with her friend. She learned that she was nervous about letting go of the relationship because of everything she would lose (the objects she kept dropping in the dream), but she felt so much freer when she allowed herself to let go of what she didn't need anymore. She later learned that horses often represent freedom and the wild spirit, and with all of these things coinciding, she finally felt confident enough to make the decision to leave her relationship.

All of those seemingly unimportant details were little markers that Lena could notice and follow. A big part of the process is learning to trust yourself and your Higher Self more and more. You could easily dismiss small coincidences in your life. You could easily quiet the small voice of your intuition in favor of logic. But by leaning in and developing a sense of trust that the wise and intuitive parts of you are there, you will need less and less confirmation from the Universe because you'll already feel strong in your instincts.

Not only is synchronicity a way for you to follow breadcrumbs on the trail to your healing, it's also a unique way that the Universe plays with you. There are so many interesting forces in the Universe, and when you feel like you are directly communicating with them, it gives you a special feeling of destiny. Being connected to your Higher Self and your intuition in this way keeps you motivated on your shadow work path, as it infuses the sometimes heavy and difficult tasks with some joy.

There are always many paths you can take and there isn't necessarily *one* right thing to do. Synchronicity can illuminate the best path at the moment, but remember that the path can change quickly. Because of that, sometimes synchronicity can lead you on a wild goose chase if you're relying on it *too* much without using your other tools. This is where you have to make sure you're acknowledging both your shadow and your connection to your body, and that you're grounding all of that exciting spiritual energy down through your lower chakras to keep yourself balanced. As long as you are taking special care and always learning how to trust yourself more, you can use synchronicity as your map to healing.

## Journal Prompts

What kind of synchronicity led you to your shadow work journey?

In what ways does synchronicity show up for you? In what ways have you dismissed it in the past?

How can you create more room for synchronicity to make itself known?

# Dreamwork

*Pay attention to your dreams. Write down your dreams. Remember your dreams. Note how you felt in your dreams.* I say this to every single client and student of shadow work and personal growth. These are things I say to myself over and over as well. The world of dreaming is one of the most potent sources of information and energy you can access. Not only does the dream world connect you to your brain and your personal history, it also connects you to the collective memory and experience of the entire world. You can dream of things far away and unfamiliar, yet those things can hold clues and brilliance that dramatically change your life. You can find patterns and recurring themes that explain who you are and how you process your experiences. Many of us have repeating locations in our dreams that represent different aspects of ourselves and our psychology.

Keeping a dream journal can help you track these recurring patterns. It can develop your ability to interpret symbolism, using that information to work creatively with your archetypes and create change in your life. You can look up and learn about common dream symbolism, but your own personal connection and associations to those symbols will always be more important. If you take your dreams seriously as a pathway for your Higher Self to communicate with you, they can help you make decisions, receive inspiration or warning, illuminate the hidden intentions of yourself and others, provide you with wise guides, and even teach you how to work with your own gifts.

# Trust Before Confirmation

Building a relationship with the Higher Self can be really difficult for those who wait for confirmation and validation before they make their moves in life. It's very tempting to wait for concrete information to tell you whether your intuition was right or wrong, but the very heartbeat of intuition is trust. When you start to trust your Higher Self without needing confirmation, your intuitive gifts can truly blossom and grow. This is when you intuitively feel like you want to stay home one night, and later you find out that there was a big car accident where you were supposed to be going. You cannot verify whether your intuition was protecting you from the accident or not, but in that case, verification may have meant getting hurt. You cannot wait for confirmation when the confirmation is the thing your intuition is trying to keep you away from.

This is the catch-22 in intuition: your intuition is usually right, but that doesn't mean you'll receive confirmation that it's right. Many times you won't. Letting go of the expectation that you need to know the outcome before you make the decision is the only way to let your intuition do its thing. Learning how to experience that trust, and having that trust be enough on its own, is how to have a healthy relationship with your Higher Self. You will certainly receive many cases of confirmation and validation, big and small, but let those things be the cherry on top rather than the one thing you're seeking.

One of the ways that I build trust with my Higher Self is by having a deal that if I have a psychic dream about someone else, I share that dream with them. I won't always know what the symbolism means. But it might mean a great deal to the person I share it with, giving them confirmation or contributing synchronicity on their own path. It may mean nothing to them, and that's okay too. I trust my Higher Self, and my dreams become more powerful and more insightful when I keep that agreement. I no longer need the confirmation if I have trust in that relationship with my Higher Self.

## Journal Prompts

Can you think of a time when you went against your own intuition because you were waiting for confirmation before you could trust it? What happened?

Why does it feel important to have confirmation from external sources before you can trust your own intuition? (Hint: This will be connected to your core wounds!)

How can you make deals with your Higher Self to build that trust with yourself?

Your Higher Self is always waiting to have a better relationship with you. They want to guide you through both your past and your future, and they are the wise one you have always been waiting for, but can never seem to find, in the external world. You cannot heal your core wounds without them, and they will bring you ever closer to your wholeness. It's important to open the doors to both your Shadow Self and your Higher Self as you continue along this journey. The balance between the two will keep you both grounded and connected when you enter the deeper world of your wounding in the following pages.

# CHAPTER 3

# • • • *The Wounded Self* • • •

I've always had a small voice inside me that whispers the same thing. That small voice has whispered this one thing time and time again to the trees, willing the wind to carry the message through the rustling leaves. She has whispered it to the sea as the tide comes in, to the thunder that echoes in the distance, and to the stars in the night sky that sparkle brighter in the cold. She's whispered it in the arms of lovers and in the confidence of friends. What is it that she keeps whispering?

"I want to go home."

When people hear her plea, they usually say either, "Okay, I'll see you later then," or "You're already home." I shake my head as that little voice becomes louder, because my physical place of residence is not my home. When she says, "I want to go home," with such desperation and longing in her voice, she means the ultimate home. Source. Creation. Love. What she really means is that she wants to belong.

Whispering such things to nature feels better for her because nature understands exactly what she means. Nature is free from the same fates of humanity she has suffered. Nature is closer to the source and pulse than she feels she is, as she feels she's been brutally ripped away from it. Her heart beats echoes of past pains, not the rhythm of the earth. Nature understands the ways that she's been hurt, abandoned, exiled from any sense of acceptance or belonging. The fates of humanity have taken her from love and belonging by forcefully pulling her from childhood before her time, by pushing her out of community when she questioned the ways of God, by rejecting her because of the way she experienced the world through the lens of sensitivity. Those pains have pushed her from the realm of humanity, exiling her to the edges, where she can do nothing but watch others belong while never being invited back in herself.

She is my Wounded Self, and more than anything else in the world, she just wants to go home again. She wants to belong.

# The Voice Calling Out from Exile

We all have that small voice inside of us, crying out to go home. Because no matter what your specific core wounds are, they ultimately come from the same emotional place. You were  exiled from "home" because of who or what you are or aren't. There is violence in exile, whether emotional or physical. Exile is the forceful separation of someone from their home, and when it comes to shadow work, this can take many forms. If the feeling of home is wholeness of the self and a natural state of the spirit, then exile is the wound that severs the self from that wholeness. The Wounded Self is the part of you scarred by that severance, and it continually yearns for home again, for belonging. For the empath, that wound is often the rejection caused by being "too sensitive" in ways that disturb others. For those who identify as queer, that wound is often the lack of acceptance from families or communities because of their innate sexuality or gender identity. For a nonreligious person, that wound can be the emotional and spiritual distance from their religious origin community due to their lack of similar belief. For immigrants, being away from their first physical homeland can be a complicated source of pain when it comes to feeling belonging in their lives now. For those who have experienced abuse, the wound is often the painful way their childhood and innocence were stolen from them, and as a result, they will always long to go back to who they were before the abuse began, to being a child who was secure and loved. No matter the circumstances, core wounds will always be connected to the painful and lonely experience of being exiled from wholeness. This rips away the sense of home and belonging, forever leaving you with that seemingly unquenchable yearning.

Those feelings create the patterns of wounding that you unconsciously operate under for the rest of your life. Yearning for belonging can drive your motivations and decisions, whether it's intentional or not. Because the wound that pulled you away from belonging is exile from home, you will always be yearning to heal that wound by finding "home" again. You will always have that little voice as well, desperate to return.

The Wounded Self is comprised of all the painful ghosts of yourself, all the versions of you that have been left behind. That drive to go home again can lead you to look in all the wrong places for it. By knowing your core wounds and the ways they play out through patterns in your life, you can find ways to heal them and find belonging again. And while you may never get the little voice to go away entirely, you can learn how to feel more and more at home in your life and in yourself.

## Discovering Your Core Wounds

Knowing your core wounds is a key to learning how to approach the Wounded Self. When figuring out what your core wounds are, keep in mind that you can have many of them. However, the earliest time that you can remember feeling severed from wholeness, from the feeling of belonging, will often hold the most energy. That one wound created a foundation for the others to build upon. Some people don't remember much of their childhoods, and that's okay too. By tracking whichever core wounds you can remember, you'll slowly follow the different threads that lead to the same wound of exile.

Core wounds can be made up of both big-T traumas and little-t traumas. Big-T traumas are the traumatic life events that define you, like intense episodes of abuse, the violence of war, major car accidents, and other dramatic events. Little-t traumas are things that seem smaller in the grand scheme of things, like invalidating arguments and continued emotional rejection. While the big-T traumas will feel more obvious, the little-t traumas often illuminate the more complex patterns that are connected to the rest. For example, maybe you have a core wound of being told to shut up by your parents when you were five. Without context, it may not seem like a big deal, and maybe it wasn't a big deal to your parents. But perhaps you had just discovered something interesting about yourself or had an important experience, and the timing of your parents telling you to shut up introduced or reinforced the message that your experience, or you, are not important and should not take up space around them. That message may connect or contribute to previous or subsequent traumas, which helps reinforce the larger web of wounded patterning. In this way, for this purpose, no core wound is too big or too small. We are not here to judge the size of your wounds. We are here to find the connections in them. That's why, at this stage, it is important to validate and witness all your wounds.

## *Journal Prompts*

Think back to the earliest time you remember feeling rejected, betrayed, or exiled for who you were and journal about it. Allow yourself to meditate on it, making sure to take deep breaths into the body, especially as you feel emotions rising.

Then, move forward in time from that wound and journal about each major experience of rejection or exile, each time you were made to feel as though you didn't belong. You'll need plenty of time for this, and make sure to take time for the small things and the big things alike.

As you're journaling, if you notice any specific physical sensations associated with the events, make a note of them. For example, maybe your chest feels heavy when you write about one wound, or maybe you can feel your throat tighten when you write about another. These are somatic clues you'll be able to use later.

Looking back, do you notice any common themes or threads in your wounds? What have you been rejected and exiled for?

## I Want to Go Home

Your Wounded Self is always trying to find ways to go back home again, whether metaphorically or literally. Feeling rejected and exiled is such a painful experience that we will unconsciously do anything to find that sense of belonging again, or maybe find it for the first time. Knowing your core wounds can not only help you discover ways to heal them, but also to become aware of the dangerous places they can take you. Your desire for home can make you vulnerable, and the wrong people or the wrong situations can take advantage of that.

Cults operate primarily through exploiting your desire to belong. They often appeal to those who have been exiled from their own family or community of origin, or to those who never had one, by promising a welcoming and loving place where they will *finally* belong. Because that feeling of acceptance and belonging is so intoxicating and healing at first, even if it's falsely presented, people will easily overlook red flags or toxic behaviors because of that belonging.

Abusive relationships are often the same way. The relationship provides an initial environment of belonging that feels expansive and healing to the person's core wounds of exile, which causes them to ignore or overlook abusive patterns. It often seems far more painful to be exiled twice than to ignore or downplay abuse in an effort to prevent it from happening again. An abuser will intentionally prey on that fear by telling their partner, "No one will ever love you like I do." The abusive relationship becomes so much bigger than merely one relationship, as it's tied to the wounds of the past and the psychological patterns within the victim.

While cults and abusive relationships are extreme examples of the pitfalls in the search for belonging, the same patterns can manifest themselves in many ways. Maybe your job tries to manipulate your desire for home by calling the team "a family" while also mistreating them. Maybe corporate greed convinces you that you just need to buy *one more thing* to feel happy and at home. Maybe your family members manipulate your decisions with guilt based on their own longing for home. These patterns can manifest anywhere and with anyone. If you are aware that it's happening, you are less likely to fall victim to it.

While it seems obvious that you may develop negative patterns from negative experiences, it is also possible to have vulnerabilities and negative patterns that ultimately come from positive experiences.

Heather lost her father, who she adored more than anyone else, when she was a teenager. Her father was a happy man who lived adventurously and his marriage to her mother was a romantic one. While her grief was monumental, her memories were joyful ones. Because of the way her grief mingled with her joy, as an adult Heather searched for partners who were adventurous and romantic, as that was her image of family happiness. This in itself is not a bad thing, but because of the enormity of her grief, Heather would fall quickly for every charming man without discernment. She was so attached to the happy-ending narrative that she wanted back, she overlooked red flags and couldn't discern when men were using her for their own selfish desires. Because of this, her heart was broken over and over, and she jumped from short relationship to short relationship, always blindly believing in the romance narrative that certain types of adventurous men played at. She invested so much time and energy in relationships that didn't truly nourish her. She was always left asking, "What is wrong with me that he didn't keep his promises?"

Heather's healing process involved examining where those patterns came from, then processing more and more layers of grief for the loss of her home and belonging in her family. She had to dig into her ideal-ized version of home and consider that her rosy memories may not beneficially drive her life decisions. The more she became aware of her desire to belong and how it connected to grief, the more she was able to work on finding home in herself. She stopped wasting her energies on impulsive flings, choosing instead to invest in herself and what her desired relationship would actually look like.

The desire to go home again is a strong and visceral one. It can pave the way for all types of wounded patterns to play out. The Wounded Self is always looking for an external savior, always waiting for someone to come and save the day. If someone has promised you a sense of belonging, the Wounded Self will be the first one to hand over your power to them. This isn't necessarily a character flaw or anything to be ashamed by either. If you have core wounds of abandonment or grief, or feel that you weren't cared for or protected in the past, you will naturally look for others to fulfill that past void in your current life. By knowing yourself and your patterns, and by getting to know your Wounded Self's needs and desires, you can begin to find belong-ing in yourself instead of looking for it in the wrong places outside yourself. Your Higher Self will be very helpful in this respect, as they are fully rooted in your true self and can help you intuit and discern whether your drives and impulses are based on your highest good or the unconscious patterns of your Wounded Self.

## The Body as a Source of Home

Consider the connection you have to your body as you examine your desire for home. While your body is your physical home for your time here, your core wound experiences may have led you to believe that your body is not a safe place to be. This is especially true if you experienced physical and sexual abuse or have been in environments that criticized your body or made you feel uncomfortable in it. There is a strong connection between experiences of abuse and physical manifestations like eating disorders, drug abuse, and chronic pain. Those experiences of abuse may have taught you that it is safer to be outside of your body, and you may have an issue with dissociating and feeling like you aren't connected to your body. Eating disorders and drug abuse are common reactions to abuse, as they are ways of attempting to control or escape the body. Because our cells remember and our bodies hold our experiences within them, not addressing the trauma within our bodies could lead to chronic pain and other issues. This is why, when working on your core wounds and shadow aspects, processing them mentally isn't enough. Bringing somatic practices, physical exercises, and active expressions into your healing is necessary so you can witness and process your experiences.

There are many people who will try to further convince you that your body is not your home through various forms of body shaming. Beauty companies are infamous for this. They point out things about the body that are unacceptable, telling you that your body cannot be considered home in its current state. But if you buy their products to fix these problems, you can finally feel at home in your body. Loved ones can also escalate this problem by being critical of your body and making you feel as though it is somehow wrong for you to exist and feel at home in your body as it is. This also crosses over into criticisms around personal expression and sexuality. These attempts, in reality, have very little to do with your body, and a lot to do with control and disempowerment. If you are not feeling safe and empowered in your body, you are far easier to control and manipulate.

Laura grew up in a family that was constantly judging and nitpicking women's bodies. She listened to the men in her family openly comment on women's bodies in movies and TV shows, and as she became an adult, she felt their judgmental eyes on her own body. Though she couldn't name it at the time, they were incapable of being around or seeing women without objectifying them, sexualizing them, or putting them down for not accomplishing the goal of being attractive in ways that met their preferences. Because of her experiences, Laura received the message that her body wasn't a safe place to be or call home because it was always open to others' criticism or objectification. She typically wore baggy clothes to hide her body and had a pattern of disordered eating. Part of Laura's healing was exploring what it means to feel grounded and safe inside her body. While she knew she could never control other people, she learned that she could work on herself and what she needed to feel belonging. Through untangling the conditioning she received growing up, and doing somatic practices like dancing and meditation, she was able to tap into her body as a source of home again. She even started playing with her wardrobe, feeling freer and safer to exist.

Examining your relationship to your body is a key to discovering home within it. No matter what has happened, your body helped you survive all your traumas. It has carried you to where you are now. This can be especially difficult to acknowledge if you experience chronic pain or autoimmune issues, which are common core wound manifestations, because it's all too easy to interpret your body as your enemy. (And taken a level deeper, to interpret your very existence as your enemy.) No matter the issues you face with your body, it deserves love and respect for how much it has survived and lived, and for how much it remembers.

## *Journal Prompts*

Think about your own little voice from your Wounded Self. In what ways does your Wounded Self cry out for home?

Where has your Wounded Self looked for belonging in the wrong places—with people or messages that ultimately took advantage of your wounding? Was it a relationship? A spiritual group? A job? Which specific wounds did they prey on?

Look back on your core wounds. Knowing what you now know about your desire for home and belonging, where do you see your vulnerabilities?

How can you protect your vulnerabilities while not closing yourself off to healing?

What are the manifestations of your core wounds? What patterns do you notice in your life that connect back to them?

How is your connection to your bfody? In what ways is your relationship with your body connected to your core · wounds?

# Lightwashing Your Wounds

Because you've found this book, you are likely already somewhat acquainted with spirituality and the quest for more. Entrance into a spiritual life usually requires practices centered around love, light, and positive thinking. We've already talked about how there is nothing inherently wrong with any of these things, but this is a good time to remind you that you cannot positive-think your way out of serious emotional trauma and core wounding. Such things need delicate and mindful untangling, with healthy respect for the reality of the human shadow. They are not to be blasted and washed out of visibility with bright lights. If one of your tangled shadow threads is red, you cannot change it to purple simply by thinking positively and announcing that it is purple. You need to apply the correct transformational process to alter the color. In that way, shadow work is alchemy.

To be burned by communities who preach the dogma of love and light, good-vibes-only, and it's-so-easy-to-create-your-own-reality ideas, is to have your core wounds retriggered and reinforced. Bypassing your core wounds and shadow work will always backfire, causing more harm. Since spirituality is all about your relationship with yourself, with nature, and with whatever you consider the force of divinity or energy in the world to be, it is inevitably connected to your sense of home and belonging. Rejecting your very real wounds and shadow aspects and demanding that you remain positive and lightwashed is simply another way to exile you from home.

# Divest from the Wound

When the Wounded Self is in pain, they don't always know what to do with it. Because they still feel the pain as if it is fresh and brand new, oftentimes the Wounded Self will turn to the source of the grief for comfort from the same grief. This is a common reflex in toxic patterns and relationships. For example, it is the impulse to reach out to your ex for comfort when it was your ex who caused you pain in the first place. It is a misplaced need for validation and healing. It's not that the impulse for healing is an incorrect one, but that your Wounded Self doesn't yet have the wisdom to find it in the right place. Your Wounded Self is so focused on home and belonging that they will go to the last place they felt the promise of it—the wound itself.

To overcome this impulse, the Wounded Self needs to be given different avenues. There is so much love and longing inside of you that doesn't know where to go, so you must be the one to provide those paths. You must learn to divest your energy from the situations that are bad for you, and instead consciously invest them in healthier ones.

For example, if you put all your energy into romantic relationships that don't last, and you're currently learning how to heal these negative patterns, you would benefit from putting your energy into your friendships, community, and yourself instead of your impulse to tend past relationships or new flings. This isn't an easy thing to do, as it requires changing a pattern that's been engrained in your brain for a long time. This is why self-awareness is essential. If you know your patterns, you can create a pause in your mind before immediately jumping into your habit. It may feel strange to turn toward friends instead of an old or new romantic partner. Your brain will want to fall back on the "easy" way, but it is the harder way in the bigger picture of your life. Developing supportive friendships is especially important in a culture that tends to overinflate the romantic relationship, insisting there must be something wrong with you if your partner doesn't fulfill every single need you have. As a result, starting or maintaining friendships as an adult can be very hard for people, so by going against the grain and putting your energy into supportive friendships, you are healing your negative patterning while also creating a fuller support system around you.

This applies to your passions as well. Think of all the energy you have wasted on negative relationships or situations when that energy could have been put toward achieving your goals or enjoying your hobbies. Many people find they lose the connections they had with friends when they enter a new relationship. Others may stop working on personal projects when they are bombarded with tasks at a job they hate. Maybe you have an unfinished novel, a blank canvas in your closet, or a trip to Europe you've never taken. While it's true that sometimes we simply don't have enough energy and capacity to accomplish everything we want, the patterning from our core wounds tends to push us into the habit of giving more of our energies to places that don't nourish us or help us grow. Those wounds make us more biased toward pain and disappointment, which not only suck the life from us, but make it harder to find joy or hope.

This is where spiritual communities and the positive thinking movement fall short. They are onto the idea that more joy and peace and hope is necessary to escape from our wounded patterns, but they preach ease and alignment as a natural byproduct of healing. There are so many messages claiming that if something is meant for you, it will simply happen. If something is in flow and in alignment, it will naturally come to you easily because you deserve it.

The truth is that your brain isn't wired for peace and ease and alignment. It's wired for survival, which is much more stressful than alignment. While you do need to transcend the negative patterns caused by your core wounds, relying on magical alignment without doing the hard and messy healing simply will not work. Overcoming trauma, changing your habits, and altering the way your brain processes information in any way takes a lot of hard work and a lot of hard decisions. It's a lot of fighting against the way you were built and the habits that are deeply engrained, against the systemic injustices that run our world. None of that is easy. None of that is peaceful. And while ease and peace are lovely results of self-acceptance and belonging, we must work for them.

# *Journal Prompts*

Your Wounded Self has you putting your energy into the source of your wounds instead of into healing them. In what ways do your specific core wounds take up your energy? Where do you have the compulsion to give your precious energy to your wounding instead of to your healing?

What goals, hobbies, or joys have you missed out on because of that tendency to focus on the wound rather than healing it?

How can you instead choose to invest in yourself, your passions and hobbies, your friendships and relationships, or your community?

In what ways are you biased toward pain and disappointment because of your wounds?

Which hard decisions (big or small) can you make to overcome that bias and accomplish what you want from your life? Most of the time, you know exactly which decisions these are but have been hesitant to make them.

# We're All Broken and Whole, All at Once

All of us are broken. In the same way that you cannot throw a glass on the floor, stare at the shattered pieces and say, "It's still whole!," you cannot be broken by your core wounds, stare at the pieces of your shattered heart and then insist that you are still whole. Can you pick up the salvageable pieces and glue them back together to create something new? Of course! You can even use golden glue like the Japanese art of Kintsugi, which repairs broken pieces of pottery to create something even more unique and beautiful than before.

Working with the Shadow Self and your core wounds is an art of acknowledging the reality of brokenness. It requires the ability to accept what has been broken, but also brings the hope that you can use your awareness and self-love to glue the pieces back together with gold. You will never be what you were before, but you will be something entirely more unique.

## *Journal Prompts*

Up to this point, how has your healing journey made you feel about your brokenness?

Has positive thinking and the search for wholeness negatively affected your ability to heal yourself? Why or why not?

Which broken parts of you haven't been invited to the table, whether by yourself, your family, your spiritual community, or others?

How can you honor your brokenness and your uniqueness?

# The Wounded Healer

While your Wounded Self might be difficult to work with, as they can become so enmeshed in their own pain, they can use that pain to shift into the Wounded Healer archetype. The Wounded Healer archetype is able to be a powerful healer only because of the unique painful experiences they have lived through. The Wounded Healer has been deeply wounded themself and makes no effort to pretend they're not touched by that pain. Many gifted healers and artists fit this archetype, and because of their deeply felt compassion for others in pain, they're able to reach people in a way others can't. They use their pain as an advantage, not a weakness.

Not only does this help others, but by also allowing your Wounded Self to have a platform for expression and transformation, you are consciously practicing radical acceptance of yourself. You are no longer denying those parts of you that hurt. You are creating a home for them within yourself, a place for them to belong. In that way, welcoming your pain home is the only way to heal it. That healing won't involve the disappearance of the pain, but an integration of it.

Your wounds give you a unique set of skills and sensitivities, and intentionally tending to your Wounded Self with this in mind will enable you to not only heal yourself, but also heal others. While your natural, protective instinct may be to lean away from your pain and your Wounded Self, only by leaning into them and allowing them to transform into healing can you embody the Wounded Healer.

## *Journal Prompts*

Which causes are you passionate about because of your own experience of pain?

In what ways do you lean away from, or avoid, your Wounded Self? How can you lean in instead?

How can you create opportunities for your Wounded Self to step into the role of the Wounded Healer?

At this point, you might be wondering why you'd want to engage your Wounded Self, as there is so much pain involved. What will you do with all that pain now that you've opened the doors to your wound? While the Wounded Self is an intense part of you that can often make change feel hopeless, by opening yourself to that honesty, by using your Shadow Self and Higher Self to see and discern the patterns of your core wounds, you will be able to access some powerful tools that require the level of compassion you've just invited in. There is still so much to be done.

# CHAPTER 4

# ••• *The Compassionate Self* •••

There was a small creek that ran between my yard and my neighbor's yard when I was growing up. A single wooden pallet served as a little bridge over the creek, even though you could easily jump over it without trouble. All around the creek and the wooden pallet, the grasses grew tall and unkempt. I often went there when I was feeling sad. I wasn't sure where to put those feelings, but instinctively, I knew I needed a separate neutral space for them. When I lowered myself to sit on the wooden pallet, toes dangling to feel the coolness of the creek, the wild grasses swallowing me up, I could disappear from the world that hurt and confused me. Here, I somehow felt that I was finally allowed to be sad. I didn't have to push away the feelings or pretend they weren't there. I could just sit in them safely where no one else could see me. I imagined my feelings being washed away by the creek as no one could judge me for them, but I didn't rush them. No one would be looking for me on the pallet hidden in the tall grasses.

The times I spent sneaking away from my life to simply feel my feelings were like small slices of luxury. A delicacy of melancholy I wasn't actually allowed to have. Even though the feelings themselves were not pleasant, having a place to let them breathe and move was cathartic enough to make the melancholy smile just a little bit.

I always walked away from the creek feeling a little bit better. While I didn't have the self-awareness to name it at the time, I was actively seeking a place to practice self-compassion. I knew I needed some space and time to simply sit with my feelings and let my compassion for my own being turn on. In a world where we are often taught persistence and resilience at the cost of self-compassion, bypassing our own struggles and sadness for our survival becomes a race and an accomplishment. But while resilience is necessary to move on, we can't truly move on without slowing down and allowing ourselves to simply be with our feelings, whether that's on a wooden pallet over a creek or in whatever room you're in right now, reading this. Your wounds need that space to exist, and you need your self-compassion to allow healing to happen.

## Give Yourself a Safe Space to Feel Your Pain

Now that you've opened up to your Wounded Self and all the ways core wounds manifest in your life, you might be wondering what else you can do with that information. At this stage, it may feel easier to log that awareness but then push most of that information away. Acknowledging your wounds and simply sitting with them to feel them is not easy, so as a result that urge to "let it go" and "toughen up" can be very strong. That's why, in this moment, you need your Compassionate Self. You need to find your own version of a safe little bridge over a creek, hidden in the grasses. Your Compassionate Self is the part of you that asks your wounding to sit and stay awhile. They not only acknowledge your pain with an open heart, but they step in to create safe spaces for that pain to process and heal. They encourage action, but it's compassionate action, the kind that is cathartic and drenched in delicate hope. An important distinction here is that your Compassionate Self not only has compassion for others, but they also have self-compassion. It is often easier to feel compassion for others than for yourself. Developing self-compassion is the only way you'll open up the doors to your healing and help your core wounds feel seen and safe enough to transform.

## Journal Prompts

What is your relationship to compassion? Would you describe yourself as a compassionate person?

In what ways do you offer other people your compassion but refuse to give it to yourself?

What might be some reasons you feel you can't receive self-compassion? Is there any part of you that believes you don't deserve it? Why?

# Sitting with a Feeling

We are not taught how to sit with a feeling just for feeling's sake. Especially when that feeling is "bad." We were taught to avoid bad things, run from them, fight them, ignore them, change them, but never just to allow them to exist. That's why such a simple concept, like feeling your feelings, is deceptively difficult. Your Compassionate Self will help you do this.

You may feel like you're well-versed in sitting with your feelings, especially if you've been on your personal growth journey for a while already. This is where I want to remind you that identifying and intellectualizing your feelings is not the same as simply sitting with them and feeling them. While it's true that a lot of shadow work is the art of excavating the *whys* and *hows* of your wounding and implementing a plan of action for what to do with that information, another important part of shadow work is simply feeling what you're feeling. Even as someone who teaches this, I still find myself avoiding it, because let's be honest—it's not fun to feel the hard feelings. When we're able to wrap our minds around a feeling, intellectualizing it and pinpointing it, we receive a hit of dopamine. There's a reward. But when you're sitting with your feelings, you don't always get that same reward. It just feels bad until it passes. The true reward of this step is that the stuck energy in your body gets to move and process, which you desperately need as a complementary tool to the mental awareness you practice.

Let yourself cry. Let yourself take an hour in bed just to process. Let yourself feel frustrated or angry without trying to control it or change it. Give your body the space to process those feelings, even if you're unsure of the why or the how. If you can allow yourself this, you're also giving your core wounds more permission to emerge, as you're showing yourself that you can hold space for difficult feelings and that you can simply sit with them and allow them to be what they are.

# Inner Child Healing

Once we allow ourselves to sit with our feelings, we often feel those feelings expand and take up more space. Experiencing this can also give us important information about the origin of those feelings, as we connect the dots that trace back to core wounds. The permission you've given yourself to *feel* proves to your core wounds that you have the capacity for them and that you can now use the information they give you. This is where you enter the world of inner child healing.

To understand how to approach your inner child, you need to understand the concept of *soul loss*. Soul loss is a term that shamanic communities use to describe what happens when traumatic events cause pieces of your soul to break away from wholeness in an effort to protect you. It's an important defense mechanism for the brain and spirit. This is the child who breaks away and dissociates during abuse in an attempt to protect the part of them experiencing the abuse. Soul loss is an acknowledgment of pain, and in realizing that there is simply too much pain for a person to process at once, it breaks away.

We all have pieces of ourselves that have broken off from wholeness. It's not our job to decide which pieces, big or small, were justified in doing this, but it is our job to reunite with those pieces. While it's true that you could probably live your entire life without reclaiming those pieces, your life and your spirit would feel incomplete. Being apart from these pieces of yourself only increases the yearning for home and makes your core wounds sting worse. Without reclaiming those pieces and understanding how to reintegrate them, you're also ignoring an integral function of your own psychology, which makes you more vulnerable to further wounding and self-destructive patterning.

Because core wounds trace back to our childhoods, when our first experiences of pain exiled us from our sense of home, many of those broken pieces of us are still children. They remain at the age of the wounding, with the personalities they had at the time. The interesting thing about inner children is that they also appear fully pure, carrying the innocence that was lost, while at the same time carrying the origin of the wound, side by side. In that way, they are fully aware of the pain they experienced while also containing an immense amount of joy and love, untouched by the pain. This makes the dynamic of inner child healing multidimensional and complex.

To work with your inner child, you can turn to a trusted shamanic practitioner or a therapist for help making those connections. However, you can work on this relationship on your own as well, especially now that you have a working awareness of your core wounds.

Simply put, your inner child needs you to understand what they didn't receive *then,* and that you can provide it for them *now.* For example, if at the time of the core wounding and the soul loss, your inner child didn't receive emotional support and wasn't believed, you now need to step in and provide your inner child emotional support and believe them. It's up to you to give them the things they didn't receive from their caretakers. This practice is also called *reparenting,* and it encourages you to step into the parental role for yourself and create systems of healing that replace the systems of neglect or pain you experienced as a child.

If you feel unsure about how to approach inner child healing and reparenting, start with the basics. What are the basics when it comes to childcare? Physical safety, food, water, rest, play, movement. You are now in charge of taking care of your inner child and they need all these things. How does your self-care rate? Are you hydrated? Are you eating well? Are you creating space for imaginative play and movement or exercise? Are you getting enough sleep? You would be shocked at how many needs this checklist addresses and balances. I like to say that we're all toddlers, and a good portion of our problems are solved (or at least managed) by a good runaround, a snack, and a nap. Prioritizing your basic needs also creates a structure for healing that proves to your inner child, and all your wounded aspects, that you're a safe place for them. Remember—you are your own parent now.

Another important aspect of inner child healing is not only identifying and finding those lost pieces of yourself, but also figuring out how to make them stay with you. Perhaps you know the age and appearance of your inner child, and you know why they broke off from wholeness, but you still can't seem to connect with them. Maybe they seem too far away still, so you're not actually connected or integrated. This is where inner child healing becomes more fun. In order to get your inner child to stay with you, they need incentive. They've experienced so much pain, and if they believe they'll only experience more pain when you start to heal your core wounds, why would they want to stay? Children are beacons of joy and awe, and it is joy and awe that drives them. You have to be willing to engage in joy *with* them, so they not only feel safe with you, but they also enjoy being with you. The best way to do this is to get to know your inner child's hobbies and interests, incorporating those into your life now. Maybe your inner child loves animals, so getting a dog or watching nature shows or going to a wildlife refuge will connect with them to make them feel seen and appreciated. Maybe your inner child's favorite color is green, so you start to incorporate green into your wardrobe or room decor. Maybe your inner child loves puzzles, so you start doing puzzles in your downtime to connect with them. There are endless options.

As a child, Daniel loved to dance and put on shows. He figured out early on that he felt the best when he was able to move as a way to express his feelings. When he reached the age of eleven, however, his father was worried about what Daniel's love of dance and theater would say to the world about his gender and sexuality. Daniel's father had a very rigid, old-fashioned way of identifying what a man was, and a love of dancing was not part of his vision of strong masculinity. Because of this, Daniel was shamed out of taking dance classes and putting on theatrical shows. He took on his father's fear and carried a paranoid sense of shame into adulthood about how he expressed himself as a man. He self-sabotaged many relationships by not being authentic about who he was and pushed away a lot of genuine love. To heal his inner child, Daniel not only needed to confront this shame that he was carrying, but he also needed to convince his inner child to stay. He started by dancing alone in the kitchen, quite literally tiptoeing into the expression of movement again. He chose songs he loved when he was younger, and little by little, started enjoying dance again. The more fun he allowed himself to have, the more he felt his inner child and his creativity returning. He eventually went back to dancing and acting in community theater. As a result of always keeping his inner child with him, he noticed his relationships changing. He felt better about being himself, because the joy he felt with his inner child was far better than the shame he received from his father growing up.

Jasmine's inner child loved to play by organizing and hosting parties for her friends. When Jasmine experienced soul loss due to abuse in the home she played in, she became antisocial and lost her imagination for hosting friends. As an adult, she felt lonely and uninspired by her life. As she worked on inner child healing, Jasmine began to reclaim her joy of organizing and hosting by creating an entire day of activities for her and her inner child. Essentially, she organized a party for her own inner child as a way to convince her that they could experience joy together. Jasmine wore her inner child's favorite color, purple, set up little play stations in her home for drawing and dancing (things she loved as a child), created a tea party at her dinner table, and had all her inner child's favorite foods. While it may seem a little silly, what Jasmine was really doing was creating a safe and joyous relationship with her inner child, and she promised her inner child she would continue doing that. Further along in her healing, she made efforts to include her friends and family in themed parties, letting her inner child be even more involved and even more determined to stay with her. While this process made Jasmine confront her abuse, it also allowed her to reconnect with that piece of her she lost.

## *Journal Prompts*

Knowing what you know about your core wounds, describe your inner child and how that piece of you broke apart. (You likely have more than one inner child, so focus on the one that appears to you most strongly.)

What did your inner child need *then* that they didn't receive? How can you give that to them *now?*

Look at the structure of your life now, including how you take care of your basic physical needs and your emotional needs. How is your inner child reflected (or avoided) in this, and how can you reparent your inner child better?

What hobbies or interests did your inner child have? What was their favorite color? Favorite food? What did they enjoy doing or learning about? How can you intentionally honor those things in your life now to incorporate more childlike joy and encourage your inner child to stay?

## Don't Forget Your Inner Teenager

Because soul loss happens many times, you can have lost pieces of yourself from any age. While inner children get the most attention in healing circles, I find that inner teenagers hold a lot of overlooked power. Your inner teenager holds the fiery, independent spirit of a person who's just beginning to understand their autonomy. They're especially important if you do not remember much of your childhood. Your inner teenager often holds the wounds that are caused during first heartbreaks, childhoods disappearing, and the harsh realities of careening toward adulthood. Inner teenagers also hold your favorite pastimes, your favorite music, your favorite hobbies, and more.

My inner teenager was a rebellious self-righteous girl with a lot of anger and hurt. Even at that time, she knew she needed outlets for all those intense feelings, so she turned to art. Painting, poetry, and writing and listening to music were the ways she coped. She channeled her rage into those art forms, which helped her survive and also create. As an adult, I can sometimes get lost in the path of neutrality and forget how important my rage and my passion for art were and are. I can sometimes forget how much anger still lives inside me, and how much I still need those outlets. By connecting with my inner teenager to engage in the things that she loved and needed, I am creating paths to healing for her because I am witnessing and interacting with her expressions. On the shadow side of my inner teenager, her rebellion and her moods can still wreak havoc in my life and relationships if I let them. So I also need to acknowledge that, letting her know that I see and feel her pain, but that she cannot run my adult life with those tendencies. Engaging with art and music, as well as working to help others and make the world better, gives her rebellion and moods a healthy job instead. Not only does this make my life easier, but by making those connections and bringing those old loves back to life, I am also bringing pieces of myself back to wholeness, making me more and more "at home" in myself.

## *Journal Prompts*

Describe your teenage self. What were they like? What were their hobbies and outlets for expression?

What is your connection to the hobbies and outlets that your teenage self had, now? Do you still engage in or enjoy any of those things?

What struggles did your inner teenager face that may have caused soul loss?

How does your wounded inner teenager try to wreak havoc on your life now?

How can you engage with them, listen to them, bring them back to wholeness, and give them a job?

# The Mother and Father Wounds

When we talk about our core wounds and the lost pieces of our souls as inner children and inner teenagers, we inevitably stumble across our relationships with caregivers at the time. Our parents and caregivers created or contributed to most of those core wounds, whether intentionally or not. That isn't to say that we should blindly blame our parents for everything, but we do need to acknowledge their inescapable influence. As I write about the mother and father wounds, keep in mind that these wounds are often intermingled with traditional gender roles that most of us have grown up with or experienced, so that's how I describe them. I encourage you to adapt the roles and identities as they fit your own unique experiences.

The mother wound is created when you did not receive the kind of mothering that you required as a child. While this is a generalization, mothering energy is typically viewed as nurturing and emotional support. It's strong protection and mama-bear vibes. It's an oxytocin-releasing hug and soothing words in times of stress. It's the encouragement to turn inward and appreciate the tender heart.

The father wound is created when you did not receive the kind of fathering that you required as a child. Again, this is a generalization, but fathering energy is typically viewed as a protective structure that allows a child to thrive. It is outward action and the net provided beneath you as you are encouraged to go out into the world. It is material stability and it provides safety. It is the presence of an ever-sturdy hand that lovingly but firmly guides you.

When either or both of your parents or caregivers didn't provide you these things, it not only helped create your core wounds in the moment, but it also created the pattern of wounding that you automatically follow as an adult. As you seek those qualities, you may continually find yourself betrayed by that quest. It's why you are constantly drawn to the same types of people who tend to hurt you in the same way.

Your Compassionate Self is the one who will help you break the cycles of your Wounded Self. When you come across pain points of the mother or father wounds, instead of replaying those wounded patterns, you can turn back to yourself and ask, *How can I mother myself in this?* or *How can I father myself in this?* By parenting yourself, you are taking your power back instead of giving it inappropriately to others—effectively breaking those cycles. Your answers to those questions might vary wildly depending on the experiences you had growing up, of course. But no matter your experience, you are turning things back toward your own wisdom and bringing reparenting into the mix.

A mother wound I see often in clients is wounding that involves caretaking and emotional expression. If your mother was so caught up in her own emotional dramas that she required you to take care of her, you likely didn't receive any type of supportive emotional space for your own feelings and experiences. Because of that, you know how to hold space for others but not yourself, so you might feel guilty or incapable of truly having your own feelings. On the flip side, if your mother was the repressed and unemotional type who preferred to sweep things under the rug, you will still have that same result—never having supportive emotional space. In both scenarios, to mother yourself would be to ask yourself, *How can I create supportive emotional space for my feelings and experiences?* Learning to associate emotional space with safety is what re-mothering really is.

On the other end, a common father wound that I often see involves structure. If a father was absent and unable to provide any type of presence or material structure for you, then as an adult, you might be unable to create structure and take meaningful action in your own life. You didn't have that modeled, and as a result, you aren't able to connect structure and safety on your own. On the flip side, having fathers who were overly controlling or aggressive in their structure with you as a child can also result in you not being able to take meaningful action. In that case, you were taught to view structure as control and maybe even cruelty, so of course you would avoid it at all costs as an adult. In either of these scenarios, to father yourself would be to ask, *How can I create structure in my life that supports me without cruelty and is able to push me into taking action steps toward the things that I want?* Learning to associate structure with safety is essentially what re-fathering is.

It is easy to judge both your parents for not providing what you needed, but also to judge yourself for feeling the way you do about them. Some people cut off contact with their parents in their healing journeys, some people bring in their parents to experience healing together, and others do everything in between. Some people have already lost their parents. The good news is that you can work on your mother and father wounds without needing to make any decisions about your actual parents. Because reparenting is about stepping into the parental roles for yourself, this is a self-defining process.

## *Journal Prompts*

Identify your mother wound. How did it come about and how does it still affect you in your life?

How can you focus on re-mothering yourself, or creating safety within emotional spaces?

Identify your father wound. How did it come about and how does it still affect you in your life?

How can you focus on re-fathering yourself, or creating safety with structure and action?

# *EXERCISE:* REPARENTING YOURSELF

Use a page in your journal. On one side of the page, list different needs you had as a child that weren't met. They can be big or small.

On the other side of the page, come up with corresponding ideas for each need you listed. What can you do to reparent yourself in that need? Note if it falls into the re-mothering or re-fathering categories, or both. Here are examples.

**Need:** I needed to be able to share how I was feeling without being told to be quiet or that my feelings weren't real or important.

**Idea:** I can give myself time each day to journal my feelings without censoring myself or judging myself (re-mothering). I can make sure that the carefully selected people I share my feelings with know my boundaries on how to handle my sharing. I can make a point not to share with unsafe people (re-fathering).

**Need:** I needed to be fed dinner and given baths in the evenings, but I often wasn't. I often went hungry or tried to feed and clean myself and my siblings with much difficulty.

**Idea:** I can make easy meal plans and set an alarm so I have a regular dinner time. I can get bath products that feel really luxurious to me so I associate baths and showers with positive self-care instead of wounding (both re-fathering and re-mothering).

Every idea you come up with connects your Compassionate Self to your inner child, creating options and pathways for healing your core wounds. Not everything will work in the same way, so experiment to find what resonates most for you.

# What You've Inherited

Whenever you're dealing with the manifestations of your core wounds and your mother and father wounds, you cannot underestimate the role of generational trauma. Lineages of trauma live within all of us, which means that some of the trauma load you carry doesn't even belong to you specifically. Patterns of energetic and psychological wounding are carried down through your line in the same way that physical genetic conditions are. This means you may have the same wounds as your mother and grandmother, or you may come up against the same exact power struggles as your father or grandfather.

One of the easiest ways to identify some of that generational trauma is by examining the roles that you were brought up in. Any role you were conditioned into fulfilling, by your family or even by your culture at large, is indicative of not only generational trauma, but also forced gender roles, religious dogma, any strong cultural phobias, and more. These types of wounding manifestations require even more self-compassion because they are patterns you didn't consent to have in your individual experience, consciously or unconsciously. These systems were forced onto you, so you need gentle love and strong protection in order to break generational trauma cycles.

This isn't to say that every role you've learned is a negative one. There is something to be said for the hugely positive force of cultural traditions and rites of passage. Keeping generational ties alive is crucial for cultural education and healthy community. I'm not here to make any judgments about any of that. I'm only here to encourage *you* to make those decisions for yourself. What is healthy for you and those around you? What is unhealthy? What generational gifts have been passed down to you, and what is generational trauma that you no longer need?

Like many people on the healing path, you may find you're the one to finally break those family cycles of trauma. It's not an easy role to take on, considering the conditioned roles you've already faced. All healing starts small, like a stone creating a small ripple on the water that eventually flows out to touch everything in sight. These small steps of generational trauma healing will flow out to touch your entire lineage: past, present, and future.

## *Journal Prompts*

What trauma have you inherited from your family line? Do you see any common patterns or symptoms between your family members, their wounds and patterns, and yours?

What roles have you inherited? What about those roles is sacred and to be protected? What about those roles has actively hurt you or no longer resonates with you?

How can you meet your generational trauma with more compassion so you can break those cycles?

To break those cycles, what decisions will you make differently than your family has historically?

## Acts of Service for Your Future Self

As we explore healing our inner children and our core wounds, we are creating bridges through time. These bridges cross years and years of our lives, but I also want you to realize that you have bridges through much smaller amounts of time as well. Every day, you have the opportunity to create healing as well as the potential to be wounded or make a wound worse. Because we tend to see our healing path as a long and dramatic landscape through our lives, we often overlook the small things that can be done every day. This is when we put off the little things that would improve our outlooks because it seems unimportant in the grand scheme of things.

One way your Compassionate Self can fix this is by reframing your daily experience to include acts of service for your future self. Your Compassionate Self knows there are plenty of little things that help you go through your day, and it focuses in on them to make your immediate future a better and more loving place for you. For example, let's say you are doing laundry, and there's a load in the washer that needs to be switched to the dryer but you're tired and would rather go to bed. Of course, the next day, too much time has gone by, so now you have to rerun the washer, and *oh yeah,* you can't wear your favorite sweater because it's still wet. Your Compassionate Self can stop you from going to bed before switching the load by asking, *How can we make life better for my future self?* Through that self-compassionate process, you switch the loads, wake up to fresh and clean clothes, throw on your favorite sweater, and your day can continue. Maybe there's a phone call you're dreading and avoiding, but every day you avoid making it, your stress grows. If your Compassionate Self steps in and gets the call over with, your future self will be so grateful that the mental strain is gone! These are really small examples, of course, but doing the small things is important. These acts of service for your future self are not meant to feel good in the moment, they're meant to show you how your self-compassionate actions create bridges to an easier and more loving future. When you start thanking your past self for these small things because the quality of your life is improving, you know that it's working.

## *Journal Prompts*

What are the small things you forget to do for yourself or that you simply neglect because it's hard to remember to make time for them? How do they affect your life?

How would your life be different or easier if you had fewer of these small stumbling blocks in your day?

List a handful of the little things you can do as acts of service for your future self.

Armed with the tools of your Compassionate Self, you're not only breaking the cycles of your core wounds, you're also stepping into a completely new world of understanding and power. You'll find that by using these shadow work methods to create bridges of healing through time, no task will seem impossible. Your Compassionate Self knows how to create supportive emotional space and structures for meaningful action, and once those foundations are laid for your inner child and your other wounded aspects, you'll be ready to take on even more of the intense dynamics of shadow work.

# CHAPTER 5

# • • • *The Powerful Self* • • •

There was a loud thump at the window. Not the sharp tick of a stone or stick hitting the glass, but the rounded, echoing sound of a feathered creature that miscalculated its flight. I rushed to look through the window, searching the sloped roof below for the injured bird. Already, my instinct to help the creature had kicked in. But instead of finding the poor thing on the roof as I expected, only small feathers were scattered about. I followed their trail to the twisted oak tree that hid the second story apartment of the Victorian house I called home at the time. The tree's branches were still naked in the end of winter. There, perched proudly on a gnarled branch, was an enormous hawk, and in its talons, a fat robin. It was shocking to see a bird of such magnitude, in a bustling city neighborhood no less, mere feet from the glass I put my hand against. It seemed to clock my presence but made no effort to move. Instead, it began the work of eating the robin, small feathers flying everywhere, as its eyes met mine again and again between bites. The scene captured me with both viciousness and beauty. The hawk seemed to challenge me to continue watching, and created a stirring in me. It seemed to ask, "Are you the predator or are you the prey?" My softened Compassionate Self felt strongly for the robin, and yet, the hawk seemed to force my inner warrior self to stand taller and take note. The dance between contradictions whirled inside me as I sat with the hungry hawk until it very decidedly flew away. The experience stayed with me long afterward. Hours later, as I left the house, there was a gift on the front steps: the tiny skull and beak of the robin, perfectly placed in my path as if the hawk had arranged it to be so. The hawk and the robin asked again: "Are you the predator or are you the prey?"

# Your Blade of Truth

The Powerful Self is the archetype that understands the role of power. It understands the roles of predator and prey. It is the part of you that has looked honestly at the ways power itself has hurt you, causing or contributing to your core wounds. It considers the ways your Shadow Self wielded power in an unhealthy manner, and the ways you can now reclaim it to empower yourself and others. While the Wounded Self required gentle compassion for its healing, the Powerful Self requires the sharpened blade of truth. There is no lying to this part of you. Many people willingly avoid working with their own Powerful Self because by working with it, you make a conscious choice to break all spells of delusion. The world will never look the same. Relationships and values might crumble. The bubble that once felt safe, that once defined your world or your very identity, will pop.

No true and lasting core wound healing can occur without popping all bubbles of delusion. Your core wounds stay hidden by operating within the cycle they were created in, and shadow work, at its essence, is interrupting cycles. Your core wounds require that blade of truth to be able to interrupt those cycles and transform into something healing and powerful.

# Power Dynamics

The further you dig into your Shadow Self, the more you reveal the hierarchies and psychological games that contributed to its creation and evolution. Exploring power dynamics in your history and psyche is a key component of shadow work. On one end of the spectrum, you are the prey, being taken advantage of or hunted. On the other end of the spectrum, you are the predator, taking advantage of or hunting others. Neither of these are considered a positive thing in civilized society, as humans are supposed to be entirely separate from beasts. This means that both have been pushed into the shadows, to remain unseen or unexamined. While the civilized world has been completely built on power dynamics and continues to run on them, it is still considered unseemly to be open about them or to examine their roots.

The positive thinking movement within spiritual circles often makes power dynamics worse, as it tends to promote the idea that one should focus solely on positive thoughts, and any experience of being the hunted or the hunter is considered negativity. While there's nothing wrong with having a focus on the positive, ignoring power dynamics—especially in spiritual or religious settings—can put you in an even more dangerous position of being hunted.

Not all power dynamics are negative. Many power hierarchies are put into place for organization, for progress, for clarity. When you are at work, you need to know who your boss is and what each person is responsible for. When you are in a family, you need to know which family member is responsible for what tasks to keep the household running. Power structures are not inherently evil. However, power structures always have the potential to become harmful because power *always* has the potential to corrupt. It is only when we remain unaware of this that we do not question the roles of those structures.

The very spectrum of power and survival is pushed into the shadows, which makes it that much more important to work with. Our goal in shadow work is to make the unconscious conscious. Power dynamics exist in every one of us, and are often at play in both our survival and our trauma responses. Our core wounds were often created in intense environments where power dynamics were at play. Our connection to home and wholeness was usually severed through a show of power. Many core wounds are created by some type of abuse from authority figures, or from individuals or groups seeking to "other" you and exile you with their influence. This means that by bringing awareness to those dynamics, you are working on healing your core wounds, and vice versa. You cannot heal your core wounds without understanding the role power played in creating them.

# Forced Silence as Oppression

While it may be societally acceptable to avoid discussion of power dynamics, in order to also avoid conflict, this concept is in itself a covert power dynamic. There is a prevailing thought that emotional repression somehow equals maturity, civility, or even kindness. Someone who does not react, is not goaded, and does not create discord is considered a stable and mature person. There is even a presumption of moral superiority in this dynamic. Many consider it a holdover from the Victorian era, when open expression (on most topics including politics, sexuality, human rights, and more) was forbidden. While forced silence has been a tactic for a very long time, the Victorians took it to the extreme—even filling their rooms with plenty of knick-knacks so during a moment of tension or when the conversation was leaning too closely to forbidden topics, one could look around the room and instead comment on a knickknack. This is an innocuous example, but it translates well to modern times. We still focus on small material distractions in conversations to avoid rocking the boat with power dynamics.

Who benefits most from forced silence? Those who have power over others. And who is hurt the most from forced silence? Those who are oppressed. When power dynamics like these go undiscussed or are not confronted, harmful cycles continue. Being aware of power dynamics and discussing them honestly with others (or at the very least, with ourselves) allows us to reclaim our own power from a healthier place. While there are countless examples of corrupted power dynamics in cultural history, especially within human rights, the same things take place in smaller situations—like inside a family. It's common for a family to know that one of the family members is an abuser, but they choose to stay silent about that abuse in fear of disturbing the peace and breaking up the family. When that happens, the abuser can continue to abuse without repercussion, while the silent victims are continually abused without relief. It's a vicious cycle that reinforces the idea that silence is equal to peace and civility, when in reality, the truth must be shouted out for there to be any hope that the cycle will finally be broken.

Consider that it might feel easy to identify areas in which you have been oppressed or felt forced into silence. This is a big step in understanding the fabric of your history and environment. It's an even bigger step to identify areas in which you have either forced others to be silent about power dynamics or have benefited from that silence. While that may be a harder pill to swallow, it's always both, and we have to face all the truths of ourselves to heal.

## *Journal Prompts*

Look back at your history, the way you grew up, and the environment you grew up in. In what ways did you feel like you were taught to be silent? About which issues or topics?

What lessons did those experiences teach you about the way the world works? (Whether they were true or not.)

How are your core wounds connected to silence or secrecy? Did those things connect to your sense of safety?

Where do you see that learned behavior of silence in your adult life? In what situations do you adhere to the idea that silence is civility? Are there any situations that make you feel especially uncomfortable in your silence?

What distractions do you use, or others use on you, to keep you from being honest about power dynamics and power struggles?

How can you open yourself more to honest observations and discussions about power dynamics?

# Predator and Prey

When I saw the scene with the hawk eating the robin, I became haunted by the question, "Are you the predator or are you the prey?" After contemplating for hours, I had my answer: I am both.

We are all both predator and prey, playing at these power dynamics. There is no escaping that. Both aspects are often shrouded in secrecy within our shadow selves, growing from the roots of our core wounds. By creating conscious archetypes of these aspects of ourselves, we bring awareness and understanding to the ways in which our core wounds manifest.

Put simplistically, your *prey archetype* represents the parts of you that have been victimized, hurt, or oppressed. Your *predator archetype* represents the parts of you that have learned how to use power to protect your prey self and keep that harm from happening again, which can be a slippery slope into the oppressor role. In this way, your predator self also holds the ways you victimize or oppress others, whether conscious or not. You must understand both archetypes in order to understand yourself, since they work together.

Too much power corrupts and creates so much distance from the part of yourself that feels pain and compassion (often, your prey archetype), that there is no longer a conscious working relationship between the two. This is when the hunter hunts without any regard for the prey. On the other side, too much prey energy without enough power creates a cycle of helplessness that is very difficult to break and hurts not only you, but also others around you.

A sense of lineage comes into play with the predator and prey archetypes. Cycles created by the oppressor and the oppressed can be passed down through generations, oftentimes without the following generations being fully aware of it. This is why working with your predator and prey archetypes can permeate both your immediate lineage and the overall lineage of the world.

Because of the interconnectedness of these concepts, working on one thing will inevitably create ripples of change throughout many things. That is the magick of shadow work.

# *EXERCISE:* CREATE YOUR PREDATOR AND PREY ARCHETYPES

In your journal, dedicate at least one page to each archetype. Start with whichever archetype feels the easiest to work with—for most people, the prey archetype is the easiest.

For your prey archetype, make a list or journal about all the ways you've been wronged, oppressed, victimized, hurt. As you do this, imagine that all these things are building to create an entirely separate entity, then use your creativity to give that entity a name, a personality, and an appearance. If you enjoy drawing, feel free to draw them instead of describing them with words.

For your predator archetype, make a list or journal about all the ways you have played the role of the hunter or oppressor. Think of all the things you do to protect yourself and your prey archetype. As you do this, imagine them building to create an entirely separate entity, then use your creativity to give that entity a name, a personality, and an appearance. If you enjoy drawing, feel free to draw them instead of describing them with words.

Keep in mind that neither of these archetypes are "negative" things. It's easy to automatically place shadow aspects in a negative space, but existence is much more complex than positive and negative. Both your prey and predator archetypes have complicated backstories, filled with trauma and survival, that required you to act as prey and predator at different times. By imagining these parts of you as creative characters, you gain some distance from them, allowing you to refrain from judging them.

## Journal Prompts

How are your predator and prey archetypes connected to your core wounds?

Which wounds activate which archetype and why? What happens when they are activated?

What habits does each archetype have in your life?

Where have these habits created destruction in your life? Be as honest as you can.

# Give an Archetype a Job

While knowing your predator and prey archetypes is an important step of gaining awareness, now that you've created them you also need to know what to do with them. Like every other part of yourself, your predator and prey need jobs. Shadow work is about witnessing all the parts of yourself, so you need to create conscious space for them to be seen.

Being a storyteller is always a productive job for archetypes. Any creative environment where they can tell their stories, unfiltered, gives them validation. That could mean writing, dancing, singing, activism for a cause, roleplaying game nights—any form of creative expression or intentional action that feels good to you. You can also use your predator archetype to protect your boundaries, and you can use your prey archetype to apply your compassion. There are many places to let your predator and prey exist, and as long as you're doing this consciously, those archetypes won't infiltrate your life in ways that are harmful to yourself or others. They will be channeled in ways that show your true power and how to wield it.

---

### *Journal Prompts*

Now that you know your predator and prey archetypes, how can you give them jobs? Which jobs can you give them so they still have ways to express themselves and their stories?

What forms of expression do your predator and prey archetypes prefer?

---

## Manipulation's Many Faces

As you work with the power dynamics in your shadow and reveal how your predator and prey manifest, consider how manipulation shows up. Manipulation occurs in all power dynamics, and in all relationships, to some degree. Manipulation is bending power for your own means. It can be overt or covert, and contrary to popular belief, manipulation isn't always malicious.

One result of necessary manipulation is survival. Many have used manipulation techniques to survive in a hostile environment, like placating an abuser to avoid further abuse. It can be necessary to bend whatever power we have available, like exploiting an abuser's emotions or habits in order to survive the situation.

Another interesting example is therapy or coaching. When you go to the root, the therapist or coach is intentionally manipulating the conversation for their own means, but it results in growth and progress for the client. Take Katrina, for example.

Katrina needed help to break unhealthy romantic relationship patterns. She always seemed to be attracted to, or became entangled with, unavailable partners—emotionally and practically. She was actively on a personal growth journey, yet still found herself in the same predicaments time and time again. Within the first two sessions, I already knew this pattern was an unconscious reaction to one of her primary core wounds: the pain and fear she felt growing up in a home built on an unhappy marriage. Her parents were not kind or loving to one another, and this early conditioning led her to believe that love equaled pain. But because she had a conscious awareness of her parents' unhappiness, she was determined to have a healthy and loving partnership instead. With this conscious, active desire to do better, she would have been unable to accept or work with her unconscious self-sabotage, instead shutting down or thinking I was wrong—derailing our work together. Her unexamined predator archetype was running the program of protection, driving her attraction to partners who would never get close enough to hurt her in the same way her parents hurt each other. This inevitably triggered her prey archetype of victimization in the end. Katrina had to reach those discoveries at her own pace, with me leading the conversation. I had to bend my observations, guiding her to notice the same patterns I noticed straight away, asking leading questions to keep her on the path of discovery. It was a longer path, but one that allowed Katrina to understand, accept, and integrate the lesson in a long-term and sustainable way. This, while having motivations that were purely good, is still an example of manipulation.

Sometimes, it can be difficult to discern someone's true intentions behind manipulation. We have all experienced the darker side of manipulation, in big and small ways. At times, we don't realize how much manipulation has taken place, or how much manipulation we have used ourselves, until much later. Learned patterns of survival manipulation can show up in our adult lives inappropriately, without us realizing it, creating more harm than good. Taking stock of your experience with manipulation helps unravel the cluster of core wound manifestations. By understanding the ways your beliefs and values were instilled through manipulation from others—whether parents, churches, schools, any institution—you may discover that you don't truly hold those beliefs or values once you remove the manipulations.

Working with manipulation in this way illuminates the struggle between survival and integrity. Sometimes, you have to stray from your moral compass in order to survive. Those decisions can wear on you and your sense of integrity. In time, your integrity itself can become warped. This isn't to say that you shouldn't have made the choice to survive, it only emphasizes the inevitability of personal moral struggles as a human in a difficult world. The more you make decisions for survival alone, the less you're able to feel your integrity. On the flip side, your survival may be considerably shortened if you go with your integrity every time. Shadow work requires you to perceive how this struggle has shaped your core wounds so you can move forward in healing them.

## Journal Prompts

How have you used manipulation to protect yourself or survive?

How have you used manipulation to cause harm, big or small?

How have others used manipulation to protect you or help you survive?

> How have others used manipulation to cause you harm, big or small?
>
> In what ways have you experienced the struggle between survival and integrity? How have those actions affected you in the long run?

# Communities and Relationships

Manipulation and power dynamics are often present in spiritual and religious communities. Behavior modification is always involved in any personal growth environment, which gives those environments more potential to create harm. This isn't always the case, of course, but it's important to be aware of the areas in which you are vulnerable. Those who would cause harm to you in this way attempt to prey on your core wounds and activate those wounds through triggers. For example, if your core wound is feeling rejected by family and feeling like you don't have a true home, then you are more likely to be manipulated by those who lovebomb you with the idea of a home and belonging in their group. After that initial wave of love, any act against you will be easily excused because you will believe that they are healing your greatest wounds. That's how the atrocities can build up.

It works the same in abusive relationships, whether romantic, platonic, or familial. Many abusers have a working knowledge of your vulnerabilities and past wounds, and will use them to manipulate you in the relationship. Whether you're aware of it or not, every relationship you have has power structures and elements of manipulation built into them. Isn't it better to expand that awareness so you can shepherd healthier relationships and prevent further harm?

## *Journal Prompts*

Look back at your experience with spiritual or religious communities, whether your experience was recent or far in the past. What were the built-in power dynamics? In what way was manipulation used for positive growth in those communities? (Perhaps you learned some positive things about yourself or the world?) In what way was manipulation used for harm?

Consider your relationships. Think back to your most important or most intense relationships. What were the built-in power dynamics? How did you or the other person use manipulation, whether for growth or for harm, to alter those dynamics?

How has your integrity been altered or warped due to manipulation dynamics you've experienced, whether consciously or unconsciously?

# Interrupt the Loop

We are often caught in power dynamics and displays of manipulation because they seep into our natural cycles insidiously. This is all learned behavior, replicating itself in new situations because it is what we were taught. History does indeed repeat itself, especially when it comes to our social conditioning. This is why someone may consistently get into relationships with the wrong people, or why another person keeps getting scammed by different communities. Our brains are always looking for the easiest route through learned patterns in the neural pathways that are the most worn and traveled. It's much easier for our brains to automatically take those same paths than to choose a different one, even if the different one is much healthier.

Shadow work—especially healing your core wounds—requires that you choose a different path. It asks you to interrupt the cycle long enough for your brain to create something better, so you're not relying on the same path that your core wounds made. In order to choose a new path, though, you first have to interrupt the loop.

# Ways to Reset

When you feel as though power dynamics are at play or when you feel your power has been compromised, reset exercises can help you interrupt the loop. Reset exercises are simple methods you can use to stop yourself in your tracks long enough to become conscious of the pattern you're in. Being able to stop yourself from cycling through the loop again allows you to step out of it, and eventually, step into something new.

## *Press Pause and Step Away*

Stopping yourself in the middle of a pattern cycle is the hardest part of the process. It isn't easy to do when you're in the thick of a situation, so begin practicing this reset exercise before you're actively inside a pattern loop. Many power dynamics and manipulation tactics involve pressured timing, because that pressure forces you to enter into the loop. Practice pressing the pause button on conversations and situations that are asking things from you or making statements about you. In charged situations, respectfully request time to process on your own before you respond or react. If the manipulation is occurring intentionally, you will separate yourself long enough to avoid the trigger. If the manipulation is occurring unintentionally, it will benefit both of you to come back into the conversation when you feel more in control of your own power.

It's also important to pause and step away whenever you're feeling confused or overwhelmed by the situation. Confusion in a tense argument can indicate that gaslighting—having your reality questioned—is occurring. If you ever feel your reality being questioned or manipulated, step away to figure it out without the adrenaline involved.

Using the pause and step away method as a habit for every big decision or discussion, or when you're feeling too overwhelmed or confused, will also help reveal the red flags in others. Those who are aiming to manipulate or control you will not want you to leave the heightened or agitated state. Their resistance to your request for a pause is a red flag. If someone intentionally puts you into an agitated state and then walks away, that is another manipulation technique that plays on core wounds and is *not* a healthy pause. Context and intention matter.

## *Verbalize to Yourself*

When you've created the time and space that pressing pause offers, it often helps to process out loud. Talk to yourself. Verbalize why you needed to step away and what parts of you were becoming triggered. Speaking it out loud also creates an opportunity to feel heard. Use this time to create more awareness of yourself and your relationships. The more you do this, the easier it will be to pause the cycle, or even break the cycle, later.

Verbalizing might sound like, "I am feeling triggered and angry at my mom. I tried expressing my feelings about not coming home for Christmas. She invalidated my emotions by calling me dramatic and then guilting me about hurting the family. This is exactly what she did when I was a kid and had any type of hard emotion or needed space for myself. She made me believe that I wasn't allowed to take up any space for myself or my feelings, and that my only job was to be there for the family. She is using the same manipulation she always has, but I don't have to spin out over this. I can instead turn to my reparenting techniques now, and I can send my mom a simple text stating my boundaries later."

## Shake It Out

Have you ever noticed how dogs shake their entire bodies when transitioning from one thing to another? We can physically shake things out too. Shaking is a powerful somatic technique that is helpful for transitions and trauma. It's a message to your body and your brain that you are now stopping one thing and moving on to something else. You can use dance or exercise or actual shaking to do this.

## Play a Game

When you're feeling overwhelmed or stuck or compromised, playing a game shifts your focus in a positive way. It can very quickly get your brain to focus on something else, interrupting the loop quickly as well. The simple matching games or word games you may already have on your phone are a great option, especially because you can play them for 5 to 10 minutes and feel totally different. This precious time creates enough distance to think about what happened in a more stabilized and un-triggered way. (This is helpful as long as you are not using extended game time to escape your problems. If this is a worry, set a timer to limit your use.)

# Embodied Power

Just as your Powerful Self is adept at identifying where misuses of power have shown up in your life, they also encourage you to discover what embodied power looks like. Some people automatically shy away from, or avoid, their power as a trauma response to being abused by power. But that doesn't work for long-term healing. Power is something we must have to live, but how it manifests is up to you. Power can be having independence in your life and the ability to make your own decisions, the willingness to express your voice and stand tall in yourself as well as in your integrity, and the knowledge that you can protect yourself if needed. Power can also be happiness and contentment and being able to enjoy your chosen life without worrying about what others will think. You are the creator of your embodied power.

## *Journal Prompts*

In what ways have you shied away from, or avoided, your own power? Why?

What does embodied power look like to you? How does your Powerful Self move through the world when you envision this?

What are some small steps you can take to get closer to that vision of yourself?

All this exploration of power dynamics and manipulation can feel tangled and murky. Because there is no absolute negative and no absolute positive, your Powerful Self is a combination of everything. They have lived and survived, developing patterns that may or may not be helpful anymore. They understand their predator and prey archetypes, and can both protect themselves and have compassion for all. Embodying your Powerful Self isn't about having the most power. It's about having the wisdom and discernment to recognize that life as a human is endlessly complex, and power is a pliable and teachable concept. Power always has the potential to corrupt, but it also has the potential to heal and create change. Your Powerful Self knows that all this truth is for healing core wounds so you can not only become a happier, healthier person, but also pass on the lineage of empowerment to others—breaking the cycles of corruption.

# CHAPTER 6

# *The Energetic Self*

I need to monitor my energy levels closely. When I get out of bed, I know that I've slept seven to eight hours. If I slept less than that, I go back to sleep if possible. Or I determine to go to bed early the next night. I know that if I don't get enough sleep, my mood, energy, and stability suffer quickly as a result.

I make myself coffee. I vary the amount of caffeine I have every day and at what time, because while coffee is one of the few things that convinces my spirit to come back to my body fully every morning, I am also sensitive to caffeine. Too much will turn on my anxiety.

Many mornings, I compulsively want to scroll through my phone or watch the news. Sometimes, I allow myself this. Most of the time, inundating my mind with that much information first thing throws off my mental health and my productivity for the rest of the day, so I restrict myself.

As I look through my to-do list for the day, I structure my schedule around priorities based on how much capacity I have, adding or removing things beyond those priorities. I take supplements and drink water every day. I work out regularly, as I feel the physical and mental benefits immediately, but I check in with my body to see when I need rest instead. I examine my support system to see if I'm craving more social support, if my loved ones need it from me, or if I need more alone time.

Some days, I spend hours meditating or reading or journaling on my own. Other days, I'll be with friends all day. Sometimes, after going out to be social, I become overstimulated and overwhelmed quickly and have to excuse myself. Then I might be alone for a few days afterward. Sometimes I realize I have isolated myself too deeply and need to reach out to my support system.

The amount of time I spend managing and regulating my own habits and nervous system might exceed most other people, to be honest. Many people don't have to worry about these things to this extent, and there have been times when I pretended that I didn't need to worry about them either. However, that's when my mental health crumbles, my creativity and productivity disappear, and I cannot regulate. I have a history of trauma, a mood disorder, some genetic factors against me, and many physical and spiritual sensitivities. These are my restrictions. They immediately affect my life, my capacity, and how I handle and process things, including how I handle and process my core wounds. If I am not honest about their existence and how to address them, then my ability to continue living and healing lessens. While it's not always fun to have these kinds of restrictions, I've come to a place where I see them as opportunities for boundaries and self-care that I meet every day with compassion and action. This is what the Energetic Self is about.

## Navigate Your Energetic Approach

After all the healing work for core wounds with your Compassionate Self and the intense truth-seeking work with your Powerful Self, you may have stumbled upon the fear that you are not capable of doing all this. Maybe you hit an emotional wall when journaling about your inner child and felt like you would never be able to break through it. Maybe you unconsciously dissociated as soon as you tried to examine how manipulation shows up in your life. Maybe your ability to process this kind of work is low right now and it drained you too quickly. If this happened to you, it's okay. This is where your Energetic Self steps in to help.

Your Energetic Self is the part of you that understands how you process energy, and knows how much you can handle as well as when and how you get overwhelmed. By tapping into this part of you, you can develop a working knowledge of your energetic capacity, influenced by your bias, your personality traits, and of course, your core wounds. As long as you have this knowledge, your Energetic Self helps you adjust your approach and methods so you won't become too activated or overwhelmed by the healing process. This allows you to continue making progress on your shadow work path. Like my experience working with my Energetic Self, you too can turn your obstacles and restrictions into opportunities for boundaries and self-care.

# Energetic Capacity

There is a reason so many personality tests examine and identify how social we are, what our strengths and weaknesses are, how we best communicate with others, and how we see the world. If we were the same, we wouldn't need these tests. But all of us are different, for many reasons, whether genetic, developed, influenced by experience or passion or pain, or simply because it's the way we came into this world. Realizing this is important when it comes spirituality and personal growth, because we can't all be expected to take the same path, need the same tools, or respond to things in the same way. Also, personal growth always involves pushing our comfort zones and growing beyond our circumstances, which adds another tricky element because our growth is largely connected to our *energetic capacity*. This is essentially your window of tolerance, the zone where you can maintain function without becoming dysregulated or overwhelmed.

If you find yourself consistently trying to operate outside your energetic capacity, the shadow work you're facing may end up doing more harm than good. Operating outside your energetic capacity might include neglecting your physical needs like sleep and nutrition, over-extending yourself to meet other people's needs instead of your own, pushing yourself through triggers to the point of mental dysregulation, activating your own stress response instead of resting, or any other actions that no longer bring a healthy return to your system.

Because shadow work is rooted in honesty with the self, being honest about your energetic capacity is also necessary. This means you have particular disadvantages and restrictions that affect your healing journey, and if you ignore those restrictions, the healing may backfire into dysregulation. This can happen all too easily. There is a strong compulsion to slide into dysregulation within the shadow work journey. Your core wounds are connected to dysfunction, and your brain may want to fall back on the things it knows best—rather than chart a new path forward. Because of this, understanding your own energetic capacity, how it developed, and how it responds becomes even more important.

Energetic capacity is not a static thing. It changes and grows as you change and grow, which is a comforting and concerning thought, at the same time. This makes a living relationship with your Energetic Self essential to keep moving forward on the path to healing.

## *Journal Prompts*

What do you know about your energetic capacity already?

How have you operated outside your energetic capacity, whether for yourself or for others? In what ways do you tend to abandon your needs?

# Intention Is Not Enough

As you're approaching your Energetic Self, keep in mind that this self does not respond to intention and magical thinking. This is where the worlds of spirituality and toxic positivity may steer you in the wrong direction by teaching you to set positive intentions through affirmations as a way to manage your energetic capacity. In theory, this is supposed to make your wishes and dreams come true.

However, your Energetic Self doesn't work in wishes and dreams. While the world of energy is a vast and magical arena, the Energetic Self only deals in the reality of how you *actually* perceive and process energy. They know where you shine, where you get triggered, the scenarios or the people that drain you of energy, and where you receive the most inspiration and healing. Your Energetic Self is a system. It is fairly direct and predictable as long as you've studied how it functions and why. Positive thinking puts so much faith into imagining a new result or outcome that it doesn't work with the actual system that would help create those changes. This creates gaps between reality and fantasy that are too hard to bridge with well-wishes alone.

When it comes to your energetic capacity, the considerations that are more important than intention include restrictions created by your core wounds and your trauma, any neurodivergent or hypersensitive traits, your physical health and chronic symptoms, the way you interact socially, and how you engage in play. The Energetic Self honestly examines all these things in your system to create a more sustainable way forward that respects the reality of your situation.

# What Your Core Wounds Created

The most important thing to consider for energetic capacity is the effect of your core wounds. At this point, you've explored your core wounds enough to see the patterns and manifestations of those wounds in your adult life. Those core wounds have created a minefield of triggers that you must navigate on a daily basis. What those specific triggers are, how explosive they are, and how many of them you have to navigate all determine your energetic capacity. Your Energetic Self encourages you to heal yourself, but they also have to navigate that minefield and keep you as protected as possible while you do so.

For example, let's say that as a child, you grew up in an environment where experiencing raised voices and yelling was a daily occurrence. In that case, your core wounds would likely include an inability to deal with yelling as an adult, as well as avoiding conflict to protect yourself from feeling that again. Because of that, your energetic capacity for working through conflict in various relationships could be a huge challenge, especially because those other people may tend to raise their voices. It may take you longer to work through conflict or be able to speak your truth in conflict. If you push yourself too hard, you may retrigger your core wounds too much, pushing your progress back. A lot of spiritual and personal growth work revolves around working through conflict with healthy communication, so you may not be able to tackle as much as books or courses or therapists tell you to. This is a restriction on your energetic capacity. When you're honest about it, you can build strategies and boundaries with others around this, while also working on those core wounds yourself.

Sexual trauma is a major core wound that affects your energetic capacity as well. Sexual trauma, especially if elements of posttraumatic stress disorder (PTSD) or complex-PTSD (CPTSD) are involved, create a lot of intense triggers in your daily life. Your capacity for many things that you may encounter on the personal growth path could be diminished. Breathwork sometimes activates body trauma when a sexual abuse survivor focuses in on it. Physical closeness in healing sessions might be challenging, or dealing with people who have traits or use phrases similar to an abuser. All this can retraumatize you instead of help you. That isn't to say you can never use those techniques, as your energetic capacity will change as you work on yourself. But knowing your restrictions is important to avoid retraumatization.

None of your core wounds are death sentences for your energetic capacity, because your Energetic Self is always trying to work with you and protect you as you heal. Instead, you need to have both eyes open about these things. If you pretend you don't have these restrictions and push forward as if they don't exist, or if you are using positive affirmations as a way to bypass their impact, you will end up hurting more in the long run. The more you work on your core wounds and see their impact in your daily life, the less charge they will have and the less triggering they'll become. Every step toward honest, sustainable healing will keep you from draining or overwhelming your capacity.

## *Journal Prompts*

Look back on all the work you've done identifying your core wounds and their manifestations in your life. What kinds of restrictions have those things placed on your energetic capacity?

What specific themes, people, or places trigger those core wounds the most? Which ones drain or overwhelm you?

In what ways have you tried to ignore or override those needs and restrictions, pretending you were fine or didn't need accommodations?

How can you instead honor those needs to protect your energetic capacity more?

# Neurodivergent and Hypersensitive Traits

In addition to the core wound manifestations that affect your energetic capacity, you also need to consider any neurodivergent or hypersensitive traits that undoubtedly have an impact. These are things you can't necessarily control that somehow alter your ability to regulate during times of growth and healing. Here are some of those traits.

- Mood swings or difficulty regulating mood and energy
- Inability to focus
- Time blindness
- Being hyperaware of other's emotions and needs
- Insomnia
- Anxiety symptoms
- Sensory struggles
- A social battery that runs out quickly or seems to operate irregularly
- Sensitivity to media and the suffering in the world
- Hypervigilance in your environment
- Restlessness or distractibility
- Fatigue
- Experiencing high highs and low lows

Let me be very clear: if you have these traits, there is absolutely nothing wrong with that. What matters is that you are honest about how these things affect you. A lot of information and advice given to people in the self-help world, in the spiritual industry and beyond, advocate blanket strategies to reach a specific outcome. If you are neurodivergent or have certain restrictions on how you experience your world, those blanket strategies will not work for you. They were not written for you. The neurotypical experience is very different from the neurodivergent. Neurodivergent systems are wired differently, tending to take in much more information at a time than a neurotypical system does. That amount of information directly affects your energetic capacity and your ability to process shadow work and healing. This means you need to adjust your own methods based on your unique energetic capacity.

If you know that you easily become mentally overstimulated, you may need to take on smaller pieces at a time. You may want to take on one chapter a week instead of binge-reading the whole book. If you experience high highs and low lows, you need to pay extra attention to creating sustainable processes you can still work with, no matter which mood you swing to, instead of committing to the heavens in a high mood and abandoning it entirely in a low mood. If you have sensory issues, you may need extra time to create a safe space where you won't be thrown off by negative sensory experiences while trying to approach these deeper parts of you. If you need more rest, rest more. If you need more support, seek more support.

This space you're creating for yourself to heal your core wounds is *your* space. You are your own advocate. You get to create your own accommodations and set your own rules. As you are doing your shadow work through these archetypes, you are the ultimate judge of what works for you and what doesn't. Your Energetic Self helps you work with rules and boundaries to keep you going on your journey, as long as you're honest about the accommodations you may need.

## Your Energy When You Enter a Room

Something happens when you enter a room. You likely scan the area, taking in the people, the environment, the overall feel and vibe. As a result, you are also likely to shift or change your own energy as a response. While it makes sense to read the room and adjust accordingly, many of us will unintentionally (or intentionally) alter our own energy to the point of nonrecognition. This is especially true for emotional chameleons and people-pleasers. There is certainly an art to changing your energy for specific purposes, but if you do it a lot, it becomes a habit that negatively affects your own energetic capacity. You can also look at this tendency as *masking* yourself. If you change yourself too much and too often, the sheer misalignment of your true self and the self you present to the world will create a dissonance within you. You end up drained of your precious, finite energy and are prevented from using it for your own creative outlets and goals.

On the other end of this spectrum, as everything is a spectrum and there's always an "other end," there are people who enter a room without reading the room at all, without shifting or changing their energy. While a confident aura, unbothered by the world, can be a great thing, shutting out too much of the world outside you actually shrinks your window of tolerance for empathy and self-growth. This affects your energetic capacity as well, because if you remain in your bubble for too long, your energetic muscles won't be built to handle what shadow work asks of us.

Guess what the biggest factor is for deciding which end of the spectrum you naturally fall on? Your core wounds. Those core wounds create the patterns for how you respond to the world as you do, whether from a place of survival or protection or reaction. Like everything else, a balance must be struck. How can you walk into a room without completely changing your identity? How can you walk into a room without ignoring the existence and experiences of others? You may find yourself on various ends of this spectrum at various times, and it's up to you to determine where the healthiest place for you is.

## Journal Prompts

When it comes to how you change your energy when you walk into a room, which end of the spectrum do you fall on? Do you tend to change your energy a lot or very little?

If you shift your energy too much, why? If you don't shift your energy at all, why?

How do your core wounds influence these patterns?

# Individualism Versus Community

Noticing how you change yourself around others leads us right into the important conversation on how individualism and community play a role in your shadow work. Community is one of the most important and powerful influences you can have in your life. Being part of a support system, whether it's a small family unit, a larger circle of friends, or even with a therapist or coach, can make or break someone's shadow work journey. Humans were not meant to be alone. The human spirit withers in too much isolation.

Modern society and capitalism do not generally support forming communities. People are kept busy with jobs and kids and homemaking, while society places an overinflated importance on romantic partnership and marriage, instead of distributing emotional needs between friends and community as well. This can lead to loneliness and isolation, while also feeling overwhelmed by the demands of partnership or parenthood. In this way, there is no support system if things fall apart. This means an environment for growth and healing is even more difficult to create. In a world where individualism is heralded as the best quality someone can have, it can create someone's downfall as easily as their rise.

Sometimes, people feel they have to give up their individualism for the sake of their own community or family. A lot of times, these people are highly sensitive people-pleasers who were taught that the needs of others are more important than their own. Martyrdom for the sake of caring for others is also not a healthy foundation of community, as you cannot fully take a place in the community if your individual needs aren't allowed to exist at all.

Both scenarios affect your energetic capacity. In many ways, your energy as a human is finite, so you naturally have to decide how to prioritize that energy. This is where your Energetic Self wants to step in to help you. How much energy do you get as an individual, and how much energy do you give to community? Sliding too far one way or the other hurts your growth, and which direction you slide indicates what your core wounds are. How can you give to both yourself and your community in a way that is balanced and healthy?

## *Journal Prompts*

Do you have a support system or community? Describe it, as well as your role within it.

If you don't have a support system or community, what kind would you like to have?

Do you overextend your energetic capacity for others, leaving no energy for yourself? Do you isolate yourself from community as a wounding response instead? Describe your patterns.

How can you balance what you need as an individual versus what you need from others and what they need from you?

How can you seek new forms of community, knowing what you know about your core wounds?

## Overstimulation Is the Enemy

If I could only choose one thing that destroys our energetic capacity the fastest, it would be overstimulation. In this era of information overload, the inescapable presence of social media, and short-form communications for *everything*—which threaten our very ability to process complex concepts and understand context—our energetic capacity is in real danger. Our brains were not meant to process huge amounts of data, like a computer might. We are still organic matter and need an organic process and approach that also prioritizes our bodies and gives our minds a break. Because information overstimulation can also create addiction (hello, doomscrolling!), it can be even harder to break those cycles, even though they actively drain us. If we allow our energetic capacity to be drained, we lose all the energy we might instead spend on our goals, or our healing, or our friends and family. Learning to identify when overstimulation is draining your energy, and how to pull back, is necessary for engaging your Energetic Self.

## *Journal Prompts*

Create a list of all the sources of information you receive throughout the entire day. Include people (bosses, coworkers, family members, kids, romantic partners, and so on), apps on your phone you interact with (like social media, news, and games), and other sources such as TV shows. Look at your list—this is likely way more information than your brain was meant to hold and process at once.

Which of these sources have a negative effect on your mental and emotional health? Which of these drain your energy so there's none left for what you actually want to do?

In what ways can you simplify or eliminate excess sources of information?

# Supportive Boundaries

Finding ways to eliminate excess sources of overstimulation and prioritize healthier outlets for your energy are all examples of creating supportive boundaries for yourself. Many of us were not taught how to create, recognize, or enforce boundaries, so mastering them can be a lifelong journey. All the work you've done so far with your Energetic Self illuminates how much boundaries come into play. It's one thing to recognize what works for you and what doesn't, but it's entirely another thing to apply that awareness with real and meaningful action. Boundaries are what will protect your energetic capacity.

Once you become aware of them, being able to verbalize your boundaries is important. If you can't verbalize your boundaries, you can't expect anyone else to respect them. Becoming comfortable verbalizing and advocating for your needs isn't always easy, and it takes practice, but the more you do it the easier it becomes. After you realize the immediate, positive benefits of taking care of yourself and giving yourself what you need, it almost feels silly to *not* advocate for your boundaries. Remember, however, that you cannot verbalize your boundaries as a way to control how someone else reacts or behaves. Boundaries are about you, not them, so you need to be comfortable and prepared to take action (like leaving the situation or ending the relationship) if others do not want to respect your boundaries.

Working with supportive boundaries is an exercise in regulating your energetic capacity and trusting your Energetic Self. It's an ongoing practice. These boundaries can shift and change as you bring more healing to your core wounds, so you must stay engaged with these parts of you at all times.

## *Journal Prompts*

How do the current boundaries in your life support your capacity and restrictions?

How do they go against what you truly need?

In what ways can you shift your boundaries to support healing your core wounds?

Even though working with your Energetic Self involves getting honest about the nitty-gritty details of your restrictions and needs, it doesn't mean restriction in all things. You can keep dreaming big and you can keep moving forward. By taking these restrictions in your energetic capacity, and giving them loving guidelines and boundaries, the journey to that big dream will be smoother and less triggering. It may take longer, but accidentally retraumatizing yourself in the name of healing will set you back further. Restrictions are not death sentences, and they're not set in stone. Let your Energetic Self use them as guideposts of your history and sensitivities, respecting their presence and adapting to the world for your highest good.

# CHAPTER 7

## • • • *The Primal Self* • • •

Tall pine trees dusted with white blurred past me as I ran through the woods. My breath was heavy but stable, creating wispy clouds in the cold air that disappeared behind me. I looked down to see my feet racing over the snow, except, there were no feet to be seen. Instead, there were four large paws covered in white fur. I was a wolf. This realization brought me into consciousness—I was dreaming. And now I was lucid. The feeling of running through the winter woods as a wolf was liberating, invigorating, comfortable. My paws seemed to know the ground before my mind did, and my body easily darted between trees before I even registered them. I heard a howl to the left of me, and then another to my right. Looking around, I saw that I wasn't alone. I was part of a pack, and together we were running and howling simply for the joy of it.

To consciously know that I was a human, dreaming of being something else, living wildly in nature, was a spiritual experience. In my human life, someone was making noise downstairs, a distant clanging that rang out in the forest. As the noise from the real world increased, my dream world became fuzzy, and I knew I was waking up. But in that strange place between dreaming and waking, the place where messages come through and the mind sees what can't be seen, I opened my eyes. My arm was outstretched before me, but it was no longer just an arm. It was the front leg and paw of my wolf self, appearing to my waking eyes. I could faintly see my human arm just underneath my wolf leg, and pushed myself to consciously lift my wolf leg without moving my human arm. In that bizarre in-between state, I played with the very fabric of reality and identity. Was I wolf or human? Being a wolf had felt so real, so right. Being wild and connected to my senses in such a primal way was almost truer than the day-to-day human routine I was waking into. Not ready to rejoin the human world quite yet, I closed my eyes, pushing myself back into the dream, to get even one more moment of freedom in that snowy forest.

## Nature in Your Body and Being

The Primal Self is your inner wolf running freely in the forest, feeling its footing before the mind does. While many of the other selves support spirit and mind, your Primal Self is the part of you connected to the earth itself and the natural cycles the earth follows. Your Primal Self is the bridge between all that is intangible and all that is tangible.

How can one deny the inherent wisdom and resiliency of the body, knowing it contains both stardust and dirt? The Primal Self acknowledges the way the body reflects what we see in nature. The riverways of our veins, the lightning electricity in our brains, the way our systems compost what we need just the same as the ground does. The body follows cycles and seasons of spring and winter, feast and famine, birth and death, the same as the earth. The body brings us closer to creation, not further, and the Primal Self celebrates this.

## Primal Instincts

Shadow work helps us trace our complicated stories back into our subconscious base natures. It helps us see how our senses and base needs are interwoven into our core wounds. Hunger, thirst, movement, breath, sex, sleep, companionship—all exist in our core wounds, as core wounds are created at the intersections of mind and body.

One of the pitfalls of positive thinking and many spiritual teachings in general is their tendency to teach bypassing the primal impulse. Many of us have been taught to override or ignore those base instincts and urges, as if what comes naturally from the body is somehow unholy. Ignoring the body and its instincts leads to dissociation. It encourages the body to hold onto energy and hold onto secrets, which creates more problems in the long run.

This disconnection from the Primal Self can be seen in many personal stories, like Dawn's experience. Dawn grew up in a very religious household where the number of restrictions in her life easily dwarfed the number of allowances. One of those restrictions was that she was not allowed to dance. Dancing was considered a sin. History has shown that dancing expresses many things, from prayer to celebration to grief, and the movement of the body is connected to divine expression. However, Dawn wasn't taught that. As a result, she grew up feeling she had to remain vigilant and rigid in her body. She pushed away what felt natural to her, for fear of getting in trouble. Over time, she developed mobility issues and chronic pain, and she always felt anxious about what she should say or not say. Dawn's healing work involved allowing herself to feel her body, move her body, experience her body. She had to reveal and work with layer after layer of repression and tension in her shadow work to feel empowered. Movement, through dancing and stretching, became an important pillar of healing for her core wounds. She now feels the divinity in her primal instincts and is breaking the cycle by teaching her children differently.

Repressing our primal instincts doesn't work. We cannot rid ourselves of something when we ignore it. It still exists. It only gets pushed down somewhere else, where it will inevitably leak out anyway, in much more harmful ways—much like Dawn's pain and mobility issues. A much healthier option is to honor your primal instincts, creating spaces for them to express safely and respectfully.

## Journal Prompts

In what ways have you been taught to ignore, override, or repress your base natures and primal instincts?

What did you notice as a result of this? What effects did that have on your mind, body, and truthful expression?

Looking at your life now, in what ways have you already broken those cycles to create a better understanding of your body? In what ways have you unconsciously continued the cycle of repression?

Describe your relationship to your body.

## Back to Basics

Healing journeys are heady. They are mental minefields. It's so easy to become entangled in the mess of the mind as you're trying to grow and evolve. This also means that it's just as easy to become ungrounded or imbalanced. Spending so much time in your heart and mind needs to be balanced out through your physical existence. Energy must continue moving and integrating to have any lasting effect on your core wounds, and you need your body to do that.

The Higher Self is often operating more quickly than the physical self, as the Higher Self is not bound by physics and rules. Your Higher

Self is having epiphanies and illuminations that transcend time and space. This is wonderful, but it also makes us forget to address the physical body, which requires more time and intention to integrate those epiphanies. Without taking care of your physical body in the healing process, your energy quickly becomes unbalanced and overloaded.

If you feel stuck, frustrated, or overwhelmed, immediately return back to basics for your body. Are you hydrated? Have you eaten? Do you need to move your body to move the energy? Do you need a nap? Remember that while you're undergoing an intensely spiritual process, you are still a physical creature. Addressing those primal needs makes shadow work and healing much more effective.

Don't let any spiritual dogma interfere with your own unique process of addressing your needs and instincts. Many teachers may want you to bypass physical needs, or seem to disrespect the fact that the body has any physical needs in the first place. They might tell you that you are transcending the body's needs through divinity by ignoring or bypassing them. I do not believe that. Our bodies are the animal vehicles of our spirits, and we are our bodies as much as we are our spirits. The body deserves to be respected and loved. It deserves to have its needs met. It deserves to experience pleasure and joy.

Addressing your basic physical needs is an important preventive measure for your healing as well. When you enter into your shadow work and core wound healing as nourished as possible, the process is easier and the integration more expansive.

## *EXERCISE:* CREATE A PRIMAL SELF-CARE BOARD

To consistently remind myself of my primal and physical needs, I use a small whiteboard as a Primal Self-Care Board. I make a list of needs or activities with boxes next to each one, and I check or star the box when I've done that thing for the day. Common activities or needs include: drink more water, get eight hours of sleep, take a walk outside, call a friend, sing, exercise, take supplements, give at least three hugs. I add things that are more specific to my needs as well. I really enjoy skincare and beauty, so I also have these things: facial, hair mask, exfoliate, and gua sha treatment. This practice not only keeps me connected to my physical body, it really helps on days when anxiety or depression creep in. I don't have to do each thing every day. But being able to check off things I did that respected my body and primal needs, even when I felt like trash, is comforting.

In your journal, write a list for your Primal Self-Care Board. Include enough options that you are able to choose at least four to five items each day. They can be as simple or as specific as you'd like.

# Going Feral

The art of intentionally returning to your Primal Self is often called *rewilding*, or as many of us affectionately refer to it, *going feral*. Going feral is exactly as it sounds. It is stripping away the social niceties and establishments to slip away into the woods, becoming a bog witch for the rest of eternity. Well, maybe not exactly, but the impulse is true. It's returning to nature for the purpose of healing and catharsis.

Many activities could be considered rewilding or going feral. Hiking, foraging, social media detoxing, hunting, herbalism, screaming on clifftops, wild swimming, intentional escape from technology, dancing in a meadow (or your backyard), gardening, learning about or hugging trees, discovering faerie portals in circles of mushrooms, sitting on grass in the sunshine, learning about wildlife and the seasons, rolling in snow, researching the history of the land. As you can see, the list is never-ending and varied, and honestly, *your* list is what matters. How *you* engage your Primal Self is most important. There should be both serious and silly options on your list, as your Primal Self is not just concerned with survival, but also joy. (How many adorable animal videos have you watched where the creatures are simply enjoying themselves?)

What does going feral have to do with shadow work and your core wounds? Your core wounds take up an enormous amount of energetic space. So much space that no form of human relationship, not even your relationship with yourself, has the proper bandwidth to fully allow and heal them. Only nature can hold all of you. Only the sky has enough space to allow all your feelings and stories and traumas to exist outside you. Only the ocean has enough depth to allow you to dive further and further into yourself. Only the trees can withstand every powerful feeling you expel from your body and record your history with unflinching steadfastness. Nature holds you in neutrality, as it holds no human judgments. This allows you to simply exist exactly as you are, as both physical body and divine consciousness. Going feral decreases the space between you and nature, creates deep understanding of yourself and what you need, and gives you access to an entire network of healing resources. I would argue that no core wound can be healed without the supportive influence of nature.

## Journal Prompts

What does "going feral" mean to you?

Create a list of what it would look like for you to go feral and return to your Primal Self. What types of activities or environments would be on your list?

Think about your core wounds. In what ways would going feral bring relief or healing to your core wounds?

Put extra thought into the aspects of your shadow work process that are too difficult to explain to others, the parts of you that never feel fully seen. How can you bring those into nature?

# What Lives in the Body

Our bodies are record keepers. Our bodies remember, even when our minds may not. In your cells, in your bones, in your connective tissue, you will find your stories as well as the stories of your ancestors and the stories of the earth. When we aren't able to process our stories and what happens to us, that energy becomes trapped in the body. When energy becomes trapped in the body, especially from core wounds, we can experience a lot of physical manifestations of those wounds in the body.

Sexual, physical, and emotional abuse can leave imprints in both our energetic bodies and our physical bodies in ways that create various blocks or conditions. Chronic pain and inflammation are often reported by trauma survivors. Eating disorders are a common physical response to abuse as an attempt to gain control over the body. Mobility issues, vocal issues, all sorts of issues, can be a response to trauma stored in our bodies. Of course, this doesn't discourage medical evaluation by any means, it simply shows that the mind-body connection is an important factor when doing shadow work.

Somatic work is used to address some of these issues. Somatic work involves gentle techniques to release stored energy from the body. This usually involves meditation and movement. Your Primal Self can help with this process, as they have a natural instinct for how to take care of and love your body. A lot of the primal expressions you've already come up with involve somatic work. Allowing yourself to freely dance might mean that your body is naturally moving in ways that let excess stuck energy out. An intentional scream or singing your favorite song over and over might be what your body needs to move in ways that clear what no longer serves your highest good. Using the following somatic exercise can help you tap into exact places where you have stored energy, so you can choose a primal expression specifically for that energy.

## *EXERCISE:*
## PRIMAL SOMATIC MEDITATION

Create meditation space where you won't be disturbed. Feel free to put on soothing music and sit or lie down in a position that's comfortable for you.

Focus on your breathing for a few minutes to settle into your body. As you breathe, bring your attention and awareness to your physical form. Let your breath create waves of relaxation energy, sweeping over various parts of your body. As this happens, lightly observe those body parts and if you feel or notice anything going on there, like pain or blocks. Most people can feel their most prominent block pretty quickly, as there will be a growing pain or discomfort. For many beginning this type of work, the first block is often felt in the throat—the place of truth and expression. If you feel tightening or constriction around your throat, know that it is normal.

Once you notice a sensation, zoom in your awareness to that area. Allow yourself to feel the discomfort or sensation. It's important that you sit with it, in this space, instead of immediately moving on to somewhere else or ignoring it. Feel the feeling. What does it feel like? Is it an emotion? Is it a memory, an experience? Use your intuitive senses to get more information. Does it have a visual? A color? A name? Develop a conversation and relationship.

You may already have the urge to move your body, touch or rub that area, stretch. (I often need to massage my heart and throat areas when working somatically.) Follow your instincts and allow yourself to move as you experience the feeling.

Once you have done this, ask the sensation what it is and what it needs from you. If you experience a throat block, you may hear that it needs to tell the truth and express itself. The block often exists because the truth of your experience has been pushed down or choked. You can ask the block if it has ideas for how to express itself.

This meditation is very personalized and can be different every time you do it. The energy may tell you that it needs to scream so it can move out of the body. It may need to physically stretch or dance or run. It may need cleansing breaths to exhale the energy out. It may need to sob uncontrollably for an hour. Your intuition needs to take the reins, figuring out how to experience, move, and release the energy from your body. All options are key expressions of your Primal Self that are responding directly to your core wounds.

This kind of work takes practice. And it can feel very uncomfortable, especially if you're not used to sitting with your feelings like this. Feel free to start small, just a few minutes at a time, building a relationship to your body and energy. It's also very important to stay true to your promises. If you discover a way to help your body move the energy while in this state, you need to follow through with it. Trusting your intuition and following through with the work is what shadow work is for, and this method can work very well, very quickly.

## Seeking Out Healthy Channels

As you loosen and move energy, on an even simpler level, somatic work gives you helpful information about yourself so you can choose how to work with that energy. To work with your Primal Self is to work with your Shadow Self. The Primal Self is neither good nor bad, for it is both. Your primal instincts can bring freedom and expression and joy, but they can also bring aggression, predatory behavior, and survival-based actions without compassion. While it seems as if those traits easily separate into good versus bad, even that distinction isn't accurate. The instincts themselves don't have moral attachments. However, you can choose to express them in either healthy or unhealthy ways.

For example, while freedom seems like an easy positive trait, it could also manifest as someone abandoning their loved ones. And while predatory behavior may sound like a negative instinct, it could also manifest as a parent protecting their child from harm. Nothing is black and white in shadow work. By accepting the nuances in your primal instincts and opening your mind to deeper contextual implications, you are allowing yourself wholeness. With wholeness follows more wisdom, understanding, and healing.

Your primal instincts relate to your core wounds, as they are both interwoven into the wound itself and the path to healing. Many do harm to others as they unhealthily act from their primal instincts, and many respond to that harm with their own primal instincts. Many people with anger issues are just a spoke on the wheel of violence, taught to be angry by others before them. You might become wounded and then continue the cycle to wound others in the same way. If you struggle with anger, you need to find outlets for it in ways that move your emotion while also avoiding harm to others. This could include an intense activity, like some form of exercise, but it could also be calming meditation. Anger itself is not bad, because anger can often be healthy—it depends on the application of it.

Some others experienced the freeze trauma response in reaction to the harm of their core wounds. While the freeze instinct is a completely natural primal instinct, it can often follow into adulthood. You might continue to freeze in situations that require your attention. If you tend to freeze, you may need a gentle outlet for your nervous system to process that response and understand it well enough to move forward. You may also benefit from intense expression as a novel way to become unstuck. Because these methods are contextual, you get to decide what works for you.

I find that watching nature documentaries can reveal a lot of wisdom about this aspect of shadow work. Seeing how different animals in various environments and circumstances respond to their challenges as they work to survive can show us how vastly and varied primal instincts show up. It also shows how simple our needs are as living beings. If you can see beyond the human container and notice how you relate to the cycles in nature, you will have the upper hand in your healing.

## *Journal Prompts*

Reflect on your core wounds. What are the primal instincts (like attacking, running, freezing, and so on) that your core wounds bring out?

How can those instincts manifest in a harmful way, to you or to others?

What are some ideas for how you can choose healthier outlets for those instincts? What can you choose instead of harm?

If you had to choose an animal in the wild that you relate to, what animal would it be and why?

What can you learn from this animal's environment and behavior that will help you with your core wounds? (This may take some research before you can answer.)

Tapping into the power of your senses amplifies your ability to experience and channel your Primal Self. Sight, sound, touch, smell, taste, all enhance our connections to our bodies and the world. I also like to add in the other two senses, proprioception and vestibular sense. *Proprioception* is the ability to track where your body is in space, while *vestibular* sense is movement and balance. Using sense information to identify wounds and also paths of healing, and to create outlets for them, is a really effective way to work with your core wounds.

# *EXERCISE:* SENSE TRIGGERS

Sense triggers are very powerful when dealing with trauma, both in negative and positive ways. Does the smell of cigarette smoke send you backward in time, to a bad memory? Does the feel of a faux fur blanket bring you a deep sense of comfort and joy? What does it look and feel like to feast? How does the warmth of the spring sun feel on your skin? Or the slight sting of cold water in the ocean? What does your body feel like as it moves through the woods? How do you respond to the sound of a busy city street, or a distant storm rolling in over the prairie? What do you feel watching a flock of birds fly across a sunset?

Understanding how your senses create an experience for you allows you to build more experiences for yourself and your healing. Take great care with your negative sense triggers and indulge your positive sense triggers. Focusing on nature-based sense triggers is best for working with your Primal Self, but sense trigger work of any kind is great for healing. Create a weekly bath ritual with scented candles and music. Fall asleep with a white noise machine, using your favorite sounds. Take a walk outside every day, taking time to indulge each sense. Throw a dinner party with the most delicious foods, savoring each bite.

In your journal, go through each sense, making a column for negative sense triggers and one for positive sense triggers. They can be as obvious or as niche as you can come up with. Once you have your list, reflect on how your core wounds show up in these lists, and how your healing might also show up. Come up with some ideas for activities to engage your Primal Self and your senses. Whenever you are feeling anxious or dissociated, come back to these ideas. Engaging with your senses is a great way to ease anxiety and return to connection with your body.

# Fire and Transmutation

We cannot talk about our primal connection to nature and shadow work without bringing up the elements. Earth is our physical body, our groundedness and stability as we move through the process. Water is our intuition and emotion, ebbing and flowing as we heal. Air is our mind, the ignition of our creativity and inspiration and movement. Fire is our passion, our anger, our expression, our very willpower.

Fire, in particular, plays a very important role in shadow work. Fire is the element of rebirth and transmutation. Because shadow work is a process of embracing and working with every aspect of ourselves, there is no place for simply eliminating one thing in favor of another. That would involve repression or denial. Instead, shadow work requires acceptance and transmuting one thing into another. Turning trauma into healing. Lead into gold. Anger into justice. Fire is the most powerful force in shadow work, and can manifest in both healing and harmful ways.

Too much fire can cause destruction while too little fire drains our willpower to live and thrive. Think of anger, passion, sex, creativity, justice, violence. Because of these extremes, fire energy can be easily misunderstood, or worse, it can be cause for people to attempt to control others. The Primal Self understands this dance of passion and control. It uses the power of transmutation to channel their fire. The habits and cycles that our core wounds create often manifest as mismanaging fire—whether that means you're on the more explosive, destructive end or the repressed, implosive end. Being able to channel your fire allows you to transmute your core wounds.

Sexual trauma in core wounds is a common reason for fire imbalance. Responding to sexual trauma can cause you to withdraw from erotic energy entirely, diminishing your inner spark and willpower. But it can also cause the reverse effect, inflaming your erotic energy and causing hypersexuality. Erotic energy, however, isn't just about sex. Erotic energy is also tension and longing, which doesn't necessarily involve sexual fulfillment, instead it can result in creative acts. This means that sexual trauma can impact your ability to navigate the art of tension and longing, as well as your ability to be creative, which is interwoven with most things in the human experience. Being honest about the state of your fire energy and how your Primal Self uses it will help healing by bringing transmutation to your core wounds.

# EXERCISE: TEND YOUR INNER FIRE

The somatic exercise you just did can be used specifically for tending your inner fire. When you settle into your body and begin becoming aware of the energy inside, focus your attention on your inner fire. Contemplate your inner fire while breathing deep and relaxing into your body. After a few minutes, you'll be able to feel where your inner fire is located. For many, it's the heart. For others, it's lower in the body. You may even notice multiple places. Wherever you feel fire energy, go with it.

Once you locate it, zoom your attention into it. What is the state of your inner fire? What does it look like? How brightly does it burn? Is it small and wavering? Is it taking up too much space or creating too much heat? Maybe it goes back and forth between the two. As you sit with the energy, maybe you feel the urge to rock back and forth or move your body a bit. Maybe you want to rub your heart chakra or tap various points of your body. Follow your instincts.

Ask your inner fire to tell you what it feels and what it needs from you, to find balance. Allow your intuition to take charge in order to hear what it says. Maybe you hear something in your head, maybe pieces of information just drop in, maybe you see visuals. It may take a few tries to develop this conversation, and that's okay. Your Primal

Self is the keeper of this fire. They tend to it, making sure it continues to burn without getting out of control. They will keep you warm and safe as long as you allow them the time and space to come back to this place.

Write down your experience and process it for a bit. Then come back to the information, reviewing what you've already learned about your Primal Self and the ways you can express energy. What does your inner fire need? How can your Primal Self help tend your inner fire? What tools and activities will be good for balancing your inner fire?

Your Primal Self is the wild self that connects your shadow to your physical body and liberates you from the heaviness of the human condition. Using them to channel your fire, explore your senses, heal your wounds, connect to nature, and express your primal instincts is one of the most powerful ways to do your shadow work. So go ahead. Go feral. Howl at the moon, become the bog witch of your dreams, befriend the crows, and bite into and savor the feast of the Primal Self.

CHAPTER 8

# • • • *The Creative Self* • • •

The cold wind whipped hair around my face as I paced, barefoot, on the seaside beach. There was a limited stretch of sand surrounded by sharp rocks covered in seaweed and barnacles. I had come to this place filled with anxiety, needing a few moments to myself. My inner shadows were haunting me, making me feel as if I was crawling out of my skin. I had been triggered by a moment of rejection. By the familiar pattern of feeling my unique voice and wisdom were novelties to others, desired and appreciated only until used up—then demonized for not exactly fitting the projected image of their desire. The same pattern of idealization and demonization had broken my heart time and time again in community, in friendship, and of course, in love. My wildness pulled them in, but so easily became an unnatural enchantment to attack as soon as they realized they could not control it, nor fully understand it and how it affected them. I breathed the sea air in deeply, willing the smell of salt and brine to become part of me, to intermingle with my humanness as we became something more. Something that eased and explained my heartbreak, something that comforted me and reminded me of my truest self.

I stopped pacing and looked out at the water. I watched waves build on the moody sea, crests falling violently inward. I carefully examined each wave, waiting to see splashes from the mermaids surely living in the cold waters of the sea. The mermaids who would surely notice that I was trapped on land, that I was secretly one of them, suffering in a strange place around strange people who would never fully understand me. Every breaking wave became a dark tail splashing, every sound and vibration became their voices, carried by water into the sand beneath my feet. I began to hum and sing in hauntingly melancholic tunes, eager to summon and answer my true family as the shifting winds took song from my lips and then carried it down the beach to join their songs. I composed this poem in my notes app.

> What if the siren's song did not lead to a man's death,
> but a man's transformation?
> And it is his choice
> to hear the truth of his nature.
> Or not.
> And should he choose to deny it,
> he would drown in his own breath,
> and blame the siren's song for his demise.
> But should he listen with courage,
> he would be reborn unto himself with new lungs.
> And swim free.

I allowed myself to stay immersed in this fantasy for a long while, as if in a trance. By the time I put my painfully human shoes back on my feet and walked away, I felt as though I shared a secret with the sea. In that way, my wounds felt seen.

## The Safety to Witness and Heal

The primal practices in the last chapter give you the opportunity to release tension in the body and connect to the earth, and creative practices offer you the gift of releasing tension in the mind and connecting to the divine. When we allow ourselves to indulge creative fantasies, the Creative Self is able to make connections between our wounding and our healing that we may be unable to link otherwise—allowing those wounds and emotions to be seen. The Creative Self is an alchemist of sorts. They intuitively know how to create channels for safely expressing pain. Your core wounds need safety to be witnessed and to heal, and since we don't always know how to find or create that for ourselves, the Creative Self takes up the task. Working intuitively with metaphor and expression comes naturally in the process of creativity, giving your core wounds gentler paths to tread.

## Thinly Veiled Artistic Healing

When working with our core wounds, at first the raw feelings that come up may be too intense to handle directly. Much like holding something so close to our eyes that we can't see or understand what we're looking at, or having a raw nerve that is still too exposed to touch, we have to find ways of working with our shadows and wounds that surround and support the wound without poking at it too much. We can create a veil between the expression and the wound, and that veil is art.

Creating some sort of artistic veil to exist between you and your wound allows more freedom to explore and express the wound without feeling as though your identity is compromised and without feeling like you're directly touching that exposed nerve. Indulging in my fantasy of communing with mermaids and writing a poem about it allowed me to explore my feelings on my core wound of feeling idealized and demonized by others. Allowing myself the veil separated the source of the wound from the expression. While the metaphors can be quite obvious and the veil quite thin, even a small amount of separation can make a big difference. Because I saw myself and my heartbreak in the sirens, I was able to see the light in the shadow and see my wound from a different perspective as it zoomed out from the nerve. I would not have had this revelation had I simply expressed my direct discontent with the situation. That's not to say direct expression isn't a tool for healing, because it most certainly is, but artistic expression provides needed perspective and exploration that we may not find otherwise.

Creativity also creates a level of anonymity and safety that you may not have if you express your wound directly. Jo experienced sexual abuse as a child from someone close to her family. At the time, no one believed her, and to this day her family exists with her secret festering within their dynamics. Jo doesn't feel comfortable or safe enough to confront her family or her abuser, knowing she won't be supported. So Jo decided that while it was the right choice not to confront them, she still needed to find ways to express herself and her wounds so she didn't fester inside. She chose to write a short fictional story under a pen name about a character much like her. She wrote a lot of her truth into this story, while also including creative metaphors and fictitious scenarios that expressed the larger themes of truth and abandonment she was exploring in herself. Her story was published in an online publication and other people witnessed and validated her story, without the pressure and exposure a direct confrontation would have brought. That artistic veil gave Jo the space to explore and validate her pain without direct harm coming her way. Because of that freedom, she was able to dive deeper into her healing process without running away scared.

Not only writing offers us an artistic veil to explore our wounds. Any creative expression is a tool for healing: music, photography, painting, interior design, beauty, film, cooking, gardening, anything. Some are not skilled with words, instead using specific colors and patterns in paintings that express their pain when they can't speak of it. There are those who use gardening or cooking as a metaphor for nurturing their inner child. I've known someone who creates beautiful makeup looks as a healing device, as growing up they weren't allowed any type of fashion or makeup and were shamed for their appearance. One of my clients did a photography series that showed the life cycle of a leaf, capturing the transformation of a small bud, to its changing colors, to its withering and dying. This series explored how they felt about aging in a world where it is looked down upon. Anything can be a vehicle for healing, as creativity itself can show up in anything. Being creative doesn't necessarily mean being an artist, so there's no need to feel pressured. Being creative is simply about using your imagination and your ideas in a way that externalizes them. The purpose here is not to create "good" art, it is to explore and process your own feelings and wounding.

## *Journal Prompts*

Think about the wounds you have that still feel too intense to be discussed openly and directly, the ones that still exist mostly in secret. While you don't have to explain them at length, use at least one word to identify them in your journal.

Now think about the ways that you're called to creativity. Do you have any art forms you already enjoy? Any avenues you haven't explored yet but have been meaning to? Whether it's as specific as writing a story down in the form of a full novel, or as vague as taking photos or doing crafts, what are ways you can express and explore your wounds through metaphor and creativity?

Which wounds would pair well with each artistic activity?

How will this type of creative expression help you understand and heal your wounds?

Once you've tried at least one of your ideas, come back to this section in your journal and write about your experience. How did it feel? Were you surprised by what you experienced? Was it easier or harder than you imagined? Note any shifts or revelations that occurred.

Sometimes, creativity is difficult to find. Maybe you don't consider yourself an artistic person, or maybe you simply feel stuck and uninspired. Either way, it's possible that in an effort to protect yourself, your core wounds are resistant to expression. In those scenarios, it's helpful to learn how to find artistry in simple and small things, in everyday moments.

## *EXERCISE:* STIMULATE YOUR CREATIVITY

Here is an exercise to stimulate creativity. Wherever you are, take a few moments to sit still. Take a few deep, intentional breaths to center yourself.

**Step 1:** Notice how and what you are feeling. The observation doesn't have to be eloquent or well thought out. Maybe you're feeling disinterested or apathetic. Maybe you're sad but don't know why. Maybe you feel hopeful. You don't have to dig deep for this step. Whatever you feel on the surface is fine and is a good place to start.

**Step 2:** Look around and take in your surroundings. What is happening around you? What is moving? What are the sounds and the colors and the smells? Maybe you're in your office, listening to the sound of phones ringing, computer keyboards clicking, and noticing the fluorescent lights casting a strange glow on everything. Maybe you're looking out your bedroom window, seeing two birds in your yard fighting over territory. Maybe you're watching a polite exchange at a coffee shop between a customer and a barista.

**Step 3:** How does what you're seeing and experiencing connect to the feeling you named before? Maybe the fluorescent lights in your office illuminate how unnatural you feel in your current job. Maybe seeing the birds fighting in your yard highlight the contrast that you feel in your apathy—are those small birds more passionate than you are? Maybe the polite exchange at the coffee shop connects to your feeling of hope for humanity. Let the associations flow, even if they don't make sense at first and even if you feel like you're forcing it. Are the things you're witnessing bringing out your feelings, creating a contrast against your feelings, or maybe even making you feel like you're not allowed to have feelings at all?

**Step 4:** Journal about these observations. Here's an example.

*What I'm feeling:* I feel like I don't belong. Like I'm out of place.

*What I'm observing:* I see a row of townhomes out my window, each alike. All the blinds are closed. It's like a ghost town. No cars. There is one singular tree in my view right now that is bright green and lush. It's a chilly day with a strong breeze that comes and goes. The breeze rustles the leaves on the tree, creating short bursts of movement and life on the street, while everything else remains still.

*Connections:* In a place where everything looks uninspired and unmoving, I am like the tree. I seem to be the only one moving in response to the wind, in response to nature and a higher force. That makes me the odd one here. But the tree is the most beautiful and lush thing I see in this view, and my ability to feel the undercurrent so deeply is what makes me stand out. I don't need to be like what is around me. I don't want to belong in a place that is uninspired. I will be the thing that moves and stirs, that is beautiful and different. I belong to a higher creative force, not the manmade buildings that all look the same.

Use this exercise often. It trains your mind to find creative connections and stretches your artistic muscles. Once you're able to more easily make these connections, inspiration will be more readily available. You'll have plenty of options for working with your emotions and wounds on deeper levels.

## Art Appreciation as a Portal

In addition to your own artistic expression, you can also explore your feelings using the artistry of others. Taking in and appreciating art is a great way to work your creative muscles, gain different perspectives, and find validation—essentially creating a portal into your own creativity. It's also a way for you to share yourself with others when direct expression is difficult. Think about all the movies and music and art that you've wanted to share with your loved ones so they can understand you better.

David was a veteran who had a lot of trauma from his service but had difficulty sharing his feelings with his wife. In exploring the ways he could try to create closeness with his wife, he began asking her to watch certain movies about war that resonated with him and made him feel less alone. He was able to communicate with her that sometimes he felt his demons more intensely and needed to feel validated and held. But he couldn't do that in direct conversation with her. She learned that on the occasions he asked her to do this with him, she could be with him, holding his hand and sharing an experience that helped her understand him. Sometimes, he was able to discuss his own experience with her afterward, and sometimes he wasn't. In any case, in those moments he felt safer with his vulnerability and closer to his wife.

Because shadow work often involves working with the difficult aspects of yourself that are harder for you or others to hold, finding artistic representation is helpful for everyone. While David used themes and scenarios in art that were self-explanatory, you don't always have to know exactly why you are drawn to certain things. Your pull toward creative works can be literal and it can also be metaphorical or symbolic. Maybe you see yourself in certain creative themes, even if you don't fully understand why. Or maybe you know why you see yourself in those themes, but you don't quite know what to do with that part of yourself yet. In any case, whether literal or metaphorical, being aware of what you're drawn to creatively is an important part of the process.

For example, I've always been drawn to vampire lore in media like books, movies, and TV shows. Whether they are deep and intelligent examples of the genre or laughably bad examples, I will enjoy them. I know that I'm drawn to this because vampires are creatures of the night, of the shadows, and I've always been interested in the shadow side, the darker side, of human psychology. I'm fascinated by elements of seduction and predation on this darker side, and also how sacrifice, innocence, and trauma play into the origin story of the vampire. It involves the predator-prey dynamic we explored in chapter 5. These stories give me space to explore those fascinations as I find metaphors for my own origin story and creative expression of my core wounds.

Another strong example I've witnessed with many neurodivergent folks is the theme of a "chosen one" in a fantasy story. There is often a character who feels entirely out of place and isolated. No one understands them and they don't fit in. Then, they discover an entirely new fantastical world, one they have been chosen to save. In this world, not only do they feel accepted, they feel acknowledged and praised. They have found their place. This is a common theme among the neurodivergent because they often feel out of place and out of step among neurotypicals. These kinds of stories give them hope and a place to explore their desires for belonging.

## *Journal Prompts*

In your journal, make a list of all your favorite, most deeply felt movies, TV shows, books, pieces of art, music, and more.

Once you have your list, look it over to find the connections. What are the common threads between these things? What are the themes? Do you tend to stay within certain genres? Do you resonate with specific types of lyrics or images?

Art works so strongly with archetypes. Now that you know and are exploring some of your own archetypes, where are you seeing the connections? In which pieces of art and in which themes do you see archetypes of yourself?

Think back on your Wounded Self and the core wounds you carry. How does your list connect to your core wounds? Where do you see your core wounds expressed in your favorite art?

What does your favorite art offer you? How does it help your healing?

# Origin Stories

In art and storytelling, we're all drawn to the origin stories of our favorite characters. Whether that character is categorized as a hero or a villain, origin stories give us context for that character's tendencies and behaviors. My favorite stories involve a character who is both a hero and a villain, or perhaps an antihero, and their complex and contradictory human nature is revealed in their origin story. I believe we are collectively fascinated by these origin stories, not just because we want to learn more about how and why our beloved character came to be, but because we want to learn more about the process of uncovering and understanding context and trauma. Diving into origin takes us into shadow work and core wounding. What were the defining moments in that character's past that colored their beliefs? Where did they overcome trauma? Where did they succumb to it? How was their innocence taken? There are so many things we can learn about core wounds by asking these questions.

In the same way we approach the origin stories of our favorite characters, we can also approach ourselves. Appreciating your own origin story as a piece of literary art is a beautiful way to work with your core wounds and your Creative Self.

## Journal Prompts

Try looking at your history in the same way that you look at the origin stories of your favorite characters. Which past events defined your character as it is now?

When and how did you overcome your trauma? When and how did you succumb to it?

In what ways do you consider yourself a hero?

In what ways do you consider yourself a villain?

How can you honor your origin story now, knowing that those defining events are tied into your core wounds?

# Travel as Medicine

Intentional travel is another wonderful way to spark your Creative Self and explore your shadow and wounds. Whether you are traveling across the world, or to a small town you've never visited thirty minutes away from home, taking yourself out of your routine for the purpose of exploration forces you to interact with your shadow and intuition in a new way. Confronted by various levels of chaos that you cannot control in your environment, you may notice both triggers and sparks of inspiration.

Traveling is also an immediate method of confronting what "home" means to you. There is excitement and freedom in being away from home—why? Those feelings tell you what you want to escape from (manifestations of your core wounds) and offer an opportunity to evaluate your life while infusing it with fresh culture and new experiences. Your Creative Self can take that fresh insight home with you to help shape your life differently. The feeling of being homesick can reveal what you value in your life, what priorities you want to hold on to, and where your comfort zone lies (for better or worse).

Because I have core wounds of feeling trapped by circumstance, I use travel to loosen those energies and find inspiration and freedom. Conscious traveling is a way I remind myself that I am not trapped, that there are always hundreds of paths before me, and that I can always make different choices. At the same time, because I'm dealing with my core wounds, I also recognize that the shadow aspect of this tool is the constant urge to run away. Having that shadow awareness brings my healing process to the forefront and forces me to examine my motives and underlying feelings.

Travel also brings you into contact with new ways to perceive what "home" is to other people. Experiencing new cultures and new traditions opens you up to compassion, empathy, education, and confrontation. It's important to be aware of the bubble you live in and find exposure outside of it, so you stay open minded enough to reflect on how you relate to the world, what you value, and how you can help. The bubble you live in can use your comfort zone as an excuse to avoid shadow work, so intentionally stepping outside it can spark your healing in a really beautiful and necessary way.

## Journal Prompts

When was the last time you traveled? How did it make you feel?

Knowing what you know about your core wounds, how does traveling, whether in a big way or a small way, connect to your wounding and shadow aspects?

How can you interact with travel, big or small, as a tool for your Creative Self?

# Design Your Home to Heal Your "Home"

While travel helps us explore our wounds when we leave, home design can help us explore our wounds when we stay. Interior design is a fun way to work with both your literal home and your metaphorical home at the same time. You don't have to be good at design to reap the benefits, either. Many of our core wounds stem from the similar experience of being exiled from whatever "home" we had. Whether that was a physical place, a community, a family, or a way of life, being intentional about your physical home now is a way to interact with your shadow and bring more healing to your core wounds. One obvious example of this is the way your style now might reflect a similar style to your parents, as a way of continuing tradition and feeling safely inside a comfort zone. Or it may reflect a total departure from their style, as a way to rebel against something in your upbringing.

Emily was raised by a mentally ill mother who had hoarding disorder. Her youth was largely spent being an emotional caretaker to her mother and struggling to adapt to the large amount of clutter and darkness in her environment. As an adult, Emily finds that she has a really hard time focusing when there's too much in her visual space. At the same time, she notices that when she is struggling with her own mental health, she leans toward creating the same cluttered spaces that trigger her. She decided to consciously work on the design of her space, choosing bright neutrals and a minimalist style with plenty of organized storage options. These choices very intentionally defied her upbringing. Because her mother didn't treat objects in their home well, with care, Emily in turn carefully chose objects and art pieces that she could treat with reverence, as sacred pieces. She also intentionally chose furniture and textiles that were soft and comforting, plenty of candles for atmosphere, and a lot of open visual space to indulge in personal luxury and self-care. While others might see her process as normal or meaningless, for Emily, decorating was a way for her to connect with her inner child and give herself the space and care she didn't receive as a child.

Mira finds that her home accurately reflects her inner landscape, and when she is putting things off in her home like going through paperwork or clutter, it connects to wounded shadow aspects she is avoiding. To honor her healing, she tries to fix something in her home, as dealing with it soothes her nervous system so she can better approach her wounding. In the home she grew up in, the only beverages they stocked were milk and orange juice, which she hated, so as an adult in her own home now, she offers her inner child multiple beverage options that they love. Again, what may seem like small choices are actually huge acknowledgments and ways to reparent her inner child.

For my own interior design, I love natural light and airiness complimented by warm and rich colors. I love to have plenty of texture and softness around, as my sensory sensitivities enjoy having things to touch. I keep things fairly clean and minimalist, as an intentional measure of mental peace, but I also create romantic vignettes of sacred items to indulge in art and beauty. I only use warm lighting and have plenty of candles. All of these choices are intentional self-care choices that surround me with openness, comfort, and reminders of my healing.

This is how interacting with your home space also interacts with your wounding. By being intentional and conscious with your past wounds, your present needs, and your future hopes, you can use your home space as a healing space.

# *Journal Prompts*

What was the style of your home growing up? Was it sterile? Cluttered? Colorful? Dark?

Looking back, how did your home reflect or contribute to your emotional experience growing up?

What is your home style today? How does it compare or contrast to your home growing up?

Think about your core wounds. How do your core wounds connect to your home, growing up and now?

What could you do in your space to intentionally work with those core wounds?

Here are some ideas.

**Never underestimate the power of blankets and pillows.** Do you have enough? Are they soft enough? Are you truly comfortable or is it just "good enough" to get by? Lacking quality blankets and pillows can indicate inner child wounding and feeling like we don't truly deserve comfort.

**Be aware of what style and temperature of lighting you prefer.** Do you like neutral light, cooler light, or warmer light? Choosing lightbulbs that are consistent with your preference can have a big impact on your emotional awareness. Are you a 'big light' person or an 'ambient light' person who feels better with lamps?

**Consider what colors work for or against you.** Which colors do you avoid because of your upbringing or core wounds? Which colors truly make you feel the way you want to feel? Modern home design uses a lot of grays and beiges, but I always encourage people to design according to their emotional preferences and not modern design. I had so many people warn me against painting a wall black, and that black wall I painted ended up being the most grounding and comforting space to me, as well as the most loved by others. I recommend looking up color psychology while reflecting on your core wounds to see how things connect. Or simply use your intuition to discover why you feel the way you do about colors.

**Notice the flow of your home.** Are pathways blocked off or too crowded? Does moving through your home feel natural? As you notice the flow of your home, notice the flow of your mind. They are connected. What does your sense of flow need from your space?

**Consider your art.** What kind of art do you like to display in your home and why? What does it mean to you? How can you engage your core wounds through your art choices in your home?

# Creativity for Your Core Wounds

All these examples of creativity are merely a handful in the realm of limitless possibilities. The Creative Self can find metaphor and expression in anything, and it's up to you to give your Creative Self the room to do it. Whether you want to take up a new creative hobby like singing or design, or you want to amp up your existing writing practice, or even make an effort to travel more or appreciate art done by others, the Creative Self will show you all the ways your core wounds need witnessing and healing.

## *EXERCISE:* CORE WOUND CREATIVITY

Reflect on using creativity as a healing balm for your wounds. In your journal, draw a line in the center of a page. On the left side, write a list of your known core wounds, big or small. Try to record around three to five of them. On the right side of the page, write down at least one creative activity you could do for each specific wound. Try to approach this exercise with intuition, as you want to feel how each activity truly aligns with each wound.

For example, let's say one of your core wounds is feeling like you have no voice after a childhood when you were often silenced. In this case, a creative activity like silently appreciating the art of others may not be intuitively aligned. For this, it would be more appropriate to choose creative activities like singing or telling a story—something that actually uses and encourages your voice that was silenced.

Once you have this list, make genuine effort to follow through with those activities intentionally, with your wound in mind. Make it sacred. And know that you can change your list at any time when you have learned more about yourself and received more intuitive hits about your expression.

Every time you engage your Creative Self, you are creating pathways to that feeling of wholeness, of "home," that your core wounds so desperately long for. In this way, you are not only witnessing your Shadow Self, you are also using your Higher Self to intuit what the expression is and what it means, acknowledging your Wounded Self, and bringing solutions with your Compassionate Self. You are exploring your Powerful Self and how those dynamics intermingle in your creativity, engaging your Energetic Self to know how and when to show up, and tapping into your natural instincts and wildness with your Primal Self. Your Creative Self incorporates every archetype for your healing. They are always waiting for opportunities to artistically weave together all the parts of you.

# CHAPTER 9

### ••• *The Healed Self* •••

I want you to imagine yourself as a capable, inspired, stable, and powerful being. I want you to imagine yourself walking through the world a little differently, with your stride more intentional and your head held higher, even if the world burns around you as you walk. The path of healing doesn't fix and change everything around you, but it does change the way you perceive, react, and exist within the world. As you let go of toxic positivity—the messages that told you to completely separate yourself from all negative things in order to transcend the evil of the world and the self—you become immune from the candy-coated delusion of mainstream spirituality. You are no longer giving your power and your reality away.

You now know what the shadow is, internally and externally, and can turn to many tools in your toolbox to address the pain of the world and yourself by acknowledging and integrating different aspects and archetypes of your being. You know how joy and creativity uplift your healing, and you turn to those things to lighten the emotional load. You won't always feel perfectly happy or perfectly at home, but you always have access to feelings of home and belonging as long as you turn inward and let your Healed Self guide you back to yourself.

# The Ever-Evolving Journey of Growth

While your Shadow Self has followed you through all the archetypes of healing in these pages, your Healed Self is the version of you that integrates all of them. The Healed Self understands how and when to use the practices that each archetype offers, in the most helpful way. Remember this: on this journey as a messy human with core wounds and trauma, there is no version of you that will ever be done healing. The Healed Self is not a finished journey nor a finished person. Healing is not a race, and there is no finish line. However, the Healed Self is the part of you that has grown exponentially and now has the tools to continue growing as new challenges and obstacles show up on your path to wholeness.

# I Am Home

How do you know that your Healed Self has arrived? You can return to your core wounds and that intense desire to belong, that yearning for home, and resist the temptation to look for it in external sources. Your Healed Self knows that you *are* home. While you might find many sources of love and validation in people, places, and circumstances in your life, relying on any of them without turning inward will not lead you to wholeness again. Everything you need to feel whole is inside of you. Wherever you go, you are home, because home is not solely external—it is your connection to yourself and the bigger picture of the Universe. Once you truly believe this, and you're able to use your tools to feel a connection to home and wholeness again, you know that your Healed Self is doing its job.

If that seems like a lovely concept, but it's hard to truly believe or apply, you may need to revisit this idea many times. That's okay. I encourage you to revisit often. There are many layers to working with the energetics of "home," and there are many feelings triggered on each layer. Here is an exercise to work with the feeling of "I am home," to help identify where you're stuck.

## EXERCISE: I AM HOME

Read the following sentence variations, speaking them out loud. As you speak them out loud, try putting difference emphasis on different words. See how this changes the meaning and how the variations sit with you. In addition to speaking them, try writing them down as well. Your only job for this part of the exercise is to feel and react. What are your first, instinctual reactions? How do the statements make you feel?

- "I am home."
- "I am my home."
- "My home is here."
- "I cannot leave home because I cannot leave myself."
- "I can always feel at home because I can always feel the connection to myself."
- "No matter where I go, I am home."

Most likely, you will feel a strong emotional response about how these statements are *not* true before you feel that they are true. This feeling is your core wounds speaking up. Your core wounds will tell you exactly why it's not true, highlighting where you currently need more love and attention. For example, if you say "I am home" out loud, maybe you instinctively feel a strong resistance to it. This might sound like "I am *not* home" or "*I* am not my home." Your brain may shout thoughts like *I'm unhappy in my marriage!* or *My family is abusive!*

or *I've never belonged here!* or *My body is definitely not a comfortable place to be!*

Once you've identified the reasons the statements feel untrue, you can use what you've learned about all your archetypes to determine how to deal with those wounds. Examining where your hurt came alive can tell you which archetype to visit, and the themes and exercises you can use to explore healing. Here are some examples.

- If your response was *I'm unhappy in my marriage!,* maybe you need to visit your Energetic Self to check your boundaries and restrictions. Then explore where your marriage is draining your energy or not respecting your boundaries. You may also want to go back to your Wounded Self to explore the patterns from childhood that inevitably show up in your marriage.

- If you thought *My family is abusive!,* you could visit your Powerful Self to pinpoint the abusive power dynamics you're experiencing.

- If you thought *I've never belonged here!,* try visiting your Creative Self and using the exercises to explore the reasons why. Maybe even do the Travel as Medicine exercise to play with the boundaries of what "here" is for you.

- If you thought *My body is definitely not a comfortable place to be!,* you can revisit your Primal Self and use the exercises to connect to your body and what it's holding.

Connect with your Higher Self to make sure you have intuitive connections to the resistance. Check with your Wounded Self so your patterns aren't self-sabotaging you. As you're noting the ways you want to rebel against those statements, it's always good to track whether any part of your body lit up or felt pain or discomfort, as you can return to somatic exercises to investigate further. Every archetype has solutions and tools for you, but at this point, it's up to you to play with those archetypes to discover how they work best with you and your healing. When you are able to speak any of these statements out loud, truly believe them, and feel the power in them, you can know you've achieved more layers of healing.

# Safety and Joy

Another reason it can be very difficult to feel truth and wholeness in the "I am home" statements is that many of us lacked safety or joy in our versions of home growing up. Experiencing safety, including both physical and emotional safety, teaches us how to stay grounded in our bodies as well as how to communicate with healthy boundaries. It also gives us the space to explore our feelings and experiences without nervous system dysregulation, like the fight, flight, fawn, or freeze responses common in many chaotic homes.

If there is no safety and no space to explore, it's also much more difficult to tap into joy. Joy is the key ingredient for any inner child healing and any manifestation or growth in general. When we don't get to experience joy, we lose the motivation for even participating in the game. Joy is what sparks inspiration and keeps us going.

Because the idea of joy can sometimes feel inaccessible, the best path to explore it starts with awe. When they feel safe, children build their worlds around awe, finding interests that spark curiosity and the drive to learn more. Your adult self can also feel in awe of things and still be open to learning, whether it's about nature or dinosaurs or marine biology or personal growth and psychology, which can clear the paths to experiencing joy again.

Lacking safety and joy also means we won't have a solid foundation built on self-esteem. Having self-esteem requires a sense of stability in the space you exist in, as well as a sense of joy and pride in who you are. While plenty of people describe low self-esteem as a moral failing or weakness of character, it really is the result of core wounding and foundational trauma around safety and joy. Those initial wounds are not your fault, and self-esteem is something that is taught, modeled, and encouraged. It doesn't simply arise, for no reason. If no one taught you to take up space, explore who you are, and have pride in your accomplishments, then of course you wouldn't naturally have high self-esteem.

The hardest part about building up self-esteem is that we usually don't have external sources to teach and encourage it. It always helps if your friends or support system are on board to encourage you, but you can't rely on external sources for internal healing. You need to be the parent and the teacher that you didn't have. You can teach yourself how to increase your safety and joy. This is where the Healed Self excels. Your Healed Self has a working knowledge of your archetypes and how they assist in healing your core wounds, so they can direct you, teach you, and tell you where to turn when you need to be built up from the inside.

## *Journal Prompts*

What does safety mean to you?

How did you experience safety, or lack of safety, in your upbringing?

How does your experience with safety reflect or explain your core wounding?

How can you help yourself create more safety in yourself and in your life? Which archetypes will help you with this?

How did your lack of safety prevent you from feeling joy? During this healing journey, are there any places in your life where you've already experienced more safety? How can you add more joy in those same places?

When have you experienced awe? What kinds of things interest you and make you feel in awe of them? How can you return to awe if you're having a hard time accessing your joy?

What do you want to learn more about to open those pathways to joy and safety?

## Shifting Belief Systems

The Healed Self is not a static creature. While its goal and wisdom always remain, the Healed Self will shift and change along with you as you shift your own beliefs. Perhaps when you first started the shadow work journey, you had one set of belief systems that slowly morphed and changed as you addressed different wounding. Maybe you discovered old beliefs from childhood that no longer served you. Maybe you even rediscovered lost beliefs from childhood that were hidden from you until you worked on inner child healing—now you want to incorporate those beliefs into your adult life. In any case, the actual belief systems matter little. You will naturally grow and change, losing and finding things as an important byproduct of transformation. This is the nature of alchemy in shadow work. Things have to change and transform. Trauma cannot be extinguished without a trace, it must be molded and transformed into something that creates joy instead of pain.

This isn't the easiest thing for humans to do, however. We are typically not very good at truly letting things go or truly letting things change. Sometimes, we stubbornly hold onto outdated and unhelpful belief systems simply because they are the ones we know and were taught. Remember how our brains always want to fall back on the easy path we've tread a million times before, even if it's not the best or most helpful path? Our belief systems are a great place to check for this tendency. Sometimes, if you're lucky, the change will happen slowly in imperceptive and subtle ways, until one day you wake up and think, *Oh! I guess I don't feel that way anymore!* But more often than not, the change requires a conscious decision and allowing it to unfold. Because of this, being honest about the belief systems you carry is important.

Still, even though *you* may be doing the work to heal yourself and change for the better, this doesn't mean the people around you are doing the same thing. Those people may even have trouble accepting the changes in you. You may find that compatibility issues arise if you truly dedicate yourself to healing your core wounds. Sometimes, if other people see you healing, it makes them confront themselves and their own core wounds. If they have no interest in facing their wounds themselves, they will not want to be reminded of them. Your belief systems may change while theirs does not, creating rifts. It's not that your belief systems are superior to others just because they've changed, however. Sometimes we simply have different beliefs, and all of us have different needs. You can't expect others to match your needs when you grow and change.

Unfortunately, because of that, the healing journey does tend to shake up relationships in ways that often cannot be undone. It's a natural part of the process, and rest assured, even if you lose some relationships or friendships along the way, your Healed Self will help.

They can support you to handle those losses and also set you up to find healthier and more fulfilling relationships on the other side.

## Journal Prompts

Do you have any belief systems you've carried since childhood? Are those systems helpful or harmful? (Often, it's both.)

Which of your belief systems have naturally shifted or changed during your healing process?

Where have you experienced walls or resistance where you know you need to change a pattern or belief, but you are finding it too hard?

What will happen in your healing process if you don't allow yourself to change?

How can you encourage yourself to change in the ways you need to, as you move forward?

## Traveling the Spiral of Healing

We know the Healed Self is never taking you to a designated finish line. Shadow work is a very layered process that takes time, years and years, to go through those various layers of growth. This means that instead of going from point A to point B, you will instead be traveling that never-ending spiral, going deeper and deeper every time you come around. Because of this, you will often spiral into new layers of the same wounds and themes. I know you will throw your hands up and say, "Ugh, *this* again?!" when you keep coming back around to the same things. But have faith. Know that just because you're coming across the same pain point and the same wound, it doesn't mean you haven't put a ton of work into that wound already. It just means you've put in enough work that you've peeled away the previous layers and are ready for a deeper one—which will encourage your connection to wholeness even more.

To help shift your perspective from a linear journey of point A (core wounds) to point B (healing, wholeness, home), instead think of the journey of the spiral as your doorway to home itself. As long as you are continuing on that spiral, you are connecting to yourself and your sense of wholeness. To stop moving and growing is to die, so in that way, there cannot be an end point. In cliché terms, it really does mean that the journey is the destination. But taken deeper, each spiral you travel contains the keys to the next layer, and then the next layer. You will always be morphing into yourself more. You will always be making decisions that make you more interesting, more stable, more joyful, more wise, more alive, and more of your Healed Self.

## Lightwork for Shadow Work

Shadow work is heavy, filled with the pain and hopelessness of our core wounds. While it is necessary to dive into those pains with our healing tools, instead of suppressing them to the point of self-sabotage, it's also necessary to leave room for the light to shine through. Without healthy doses of light, humor, and levity, the shadow work journey can pull you into the dark depths of jadedness, preventing you from knowing which direction the surface is anymore. If you lose your ability to navigate those waters, you also lose your ability to create meaningful healing.

What in your life brings you light? What makes you feel hopeful and positive? What helps you remember where the surface is, so you can enjoy the simple warmth of the sun when the depths become too cold? How can you share light and kindness with others? These things that help you connect with the light can be as spiritual or as nonspiritual as you'd like. Maybe you have a special place in your heart for those positive affirmations, or crystals, or energy healing, or community service. Maybe your pets and your kids bring you joy. Maybe it's comedy shows or thrifting or hiking or flower arrangements. It doesn't matter what brings you light, it only matters that it brings you joy.

## *Journal Prompts*

Have you felt the heaviness of shadow work, perhaps making you feel jaded? Where has it come up the most?

What kind of lightwork would work best for you? What activities (both spiritual and nonspiritual) bring you joy? How can you intentionally incorporate them into your shadow work?

## Synchronicity Comes Back Around

A good way to incorporate more light into your shadow work journey, which also helps measure your progress, is to track the instances of synchronicity you experience as you go through life. Recall the work with synchronicity that you did with your Higher Self. Synchronicities happen when you're on the right path or are being nudged in a particular direction. Making sure to acknowledge synchronicity reinforces your relationship with your intuition and your Higher Self. It's also a fun way for your Healed Self to take stock of the work you've done and the direction you are taking.

# Self-Talk: What Are You Saying?

Our brains are beautiful, silly, brilliant, feral little goblins inside us. They are constantly reacting and talking to you, but most people let their self-talk slide by without paying much attention. Your self-talk is your true measure of progress, however, as it shows how well your Healed Self is doing their job.

How often is your self-talk critical, negative, or depressing? How many negative thoughts do you think about yourself throughout your day and what do you do about them? The presence of this kind of self-talk isn't bad, in itself. We all have negative and cruel self-talk. But your Healed Self is the one who tracks this self-talk, and then asks the question, "Which of my wounds is expressing themselves in that hurtful thought?" When you can recognize your cruel self-talk as a cry for recognition from your Wounded Self, you can acknowledge that thought with compassion, then direct it toward a more healing action, instead of letting it rot inside you. It's hard to do this at first, as most of our self-talk goes unnoticed or unanswered. But the more you practice, the more you will realize that you automatically respond to critical self-talk with healing self-talk, and as time goes on, your critical self-talk will happen less and less.

I still experience a lot of negative self-talk, just like anyone else. As I was writing this book, I sometimes had the negative thought, *This isn't good enough. You're not good enough.* But instead of letting it tear me down to the point of not writing, I acknowledged that my Wounded Self, and my core wound of not feeling like my talents could be seen or appreciated, were speaking up. I soothed myself with self-compassion, understanding the pattern and the impulse for that kind of self-talk.

To reparent my inner child, I reassured myself that my talents are seen and appreciated, but even more, I assured my inner child that it doesn't matter if her gifts are seen as good enough or not. I told her she would be loved no matter what, and the mere act of writing and creating something for the world is enough. It is brave and powerful, and other people's reactions to it are less important.

These things didn't make all my self-doubt go away, especially because artists are often the most critical of themselves. But witnessing and reparenting the wound allowed me to return to writing with more inner confidence. The acknowledgment and redirection of self-talk was offered by my Healed Self.

## *Journal Prompt*

How aware are you of your own self-talk? How much of your self-talk is critical, and what kind of things does it say?

Which wounds of yours are the true authors of those negative, critical thoughts?

How can you acknowledge those wounds and redirect your self-talk to create healing instead of doubt?

Your Healed Self is the culmination of all the awareness you've built throughout this book. They are always prepared to help, with a self-compassionate redirect when you're feeling triggered, a dose of powerful truth when you need to slice through delusion, a list of ideas to help you release stuck energy in your body, and endless inspiration to channel your light and shadow through creativity. Your Healed Self knows, and is, all of your archetypes integrated into the sure-footed adventurer who not only endlessly searches for healing but also knows that no matter where they go, they are home.

# *Conclusion*

Following the road of shadow work isn't easy, and the dark twists and turns and gnarled roots coming up from the ground to trip you up certainly don't make it easier. Your individual path differs from mine and anyone else's, but using your archetypes as healing touchstones will always keep you from straying too far away from wholeness as you navigate the steps. Each of your archetypes holds undying wisdom for you when you need it, and they all have messages for you to hold onto when things get tough.

Your Shadow Self wants you to know that having a shadow isn't bad or anything to be ashamed about. They want you to remember that just as they hold the secrets of you and your history that you may not want to illuminate, they also hold the secret brilliance of gifts that are tangled up in trauma. It is always worth it to create a healthy relationship with your shadow.

Your Higher Self wants you to know that you always have access to divine channels of intuition and joy. They will always be there, ready to work with you on your intuitive senses and how to use them on your shadow work path.

Your Wounded Self wants you to know that there are secret pockets of pain within you that will always be aching for home and belonging. They want you to see and validate them, illuminating the wounded history you have and the seeds of trauma planted within you.

Your Compassionate Self wants you to know that you can meet those wounds with the gentleness of a soft word and the warm embrace that an inner child needs through the reparenting process. They encourage you to hold the type of space for yourself that feels easy to hold for others, but so difficult to turn inward. They want to give you the presence of the mothering and fathering that you needed then, now.

Your Powerful Self wants you to know that you can always see your world with pure and sharp clarity, piercing through any bubbles of delusion with the sharp sword of truth. They will always teach you how to see through manipulations and power dynamics in your life so you can protect yourself.

Your Energetic Self wants you to know that you always have the ability to examine and shift your capacity to better accommodate any needs and restrictions you may have that would get in the way of your healing. They want to remind you that you are in charge of your boundaries and that you can shift them whenever you need to.

Your Primal Self wants you to know that your primal instincts and urges to connect with your body are powerful and necessary. They will always encourage you to move and process what you're feeling, disappear into nature and howl with the wolves as you release all the excess tension in your body.

Your Creative Self wants you to know that you have an endless supply of creative energy and healing inside you, as long as you give it the time and space to flow. They believe in your ability to channel your wounds and healing process into works of art, no matter what form that art takes.

Your Healed Self wants you to know that you have everything you need inside you to use your archetypes as vehicles of healing and wholeness. They will remind you how to direct your energy and focus when different struggles come up, always pointing you in the right direction.

While that feeling of yearning for home, for belonging, may never dissipate entirely, the shadow work journey with your archetypes provides you pathways for connecting to more and more pieces of yourself, bringing you closer and closer to wholeness. All the work you've done on your core wounds to understand the seeds of trauma, and the complex root systems those seeds grew into, gives you the knowledge and power to know that you *are* home. You are home, and as long as you keep your connection to yourself alive through consistent self-reflection and meaningful action, you will always be home.

# • • • *Acknowledgments* • • •

First and foremost, I want to thank every reader and every client who has supported my work in the world. Your stories and experiences keep me motivated and inspired to do this. Whenever I get caught up in my own life or feel jaded by the industry, it's always you who get me back on track.

Thank you to my amazing editor, Jennye Garibaldi, for always being an ally and advocate, supporting me in my journey to this point. Thanks to the whole team at New Harbinger Publications for seeing my books into the world and contributing your knowledge and expertise.

To my soul sisters and peers Erin and Pam who have always held me in my shadow work journey with clear insight, sharp perception, and levity. To my partner, D, who has given me so much love, joy, and support as I wrote this book—you're my rock and my anchor. I'm not sure where I would be without this community and support system. I'm grateful for all of you every day.

To the countless teachers, healers, and community leaders I've witnessed and learned from in the last decade-plus, who have helped me shape who I am and what I'm here to do, I see all of you. You've all touched me deeply in many ways.

**Ora North** is a spiritual teacher and mental health advocate. While very involved in the spiritual community, North does not subscribe to the "love and light" or "good vibes only" mentality that can often whitewash or bypass the very real struggles of the marginalized. Because of this, her focus is on shadow work and promoting the acceptance and validation of all our feelings—not just the positive ones—as tools for growth. She is author of *I Don't Want to Be an Empath Anymore* and *Mood Magick*.

# MORE BOOKS for the SPIRITUAL SEEKER

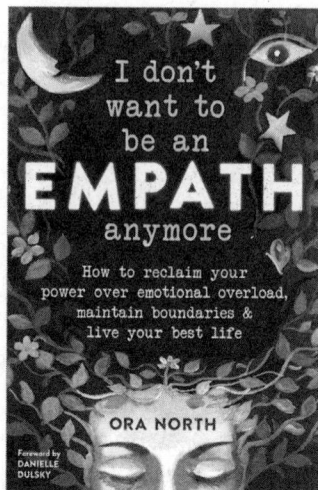

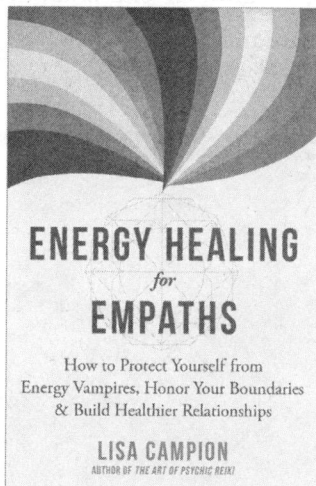

new**harbinger**publications

REVEAL PRESS